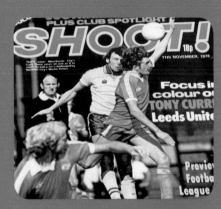

Conker Editions Ltd
22 Cosby Road
Littlethorpe
Leicester
LE19 2HF
Email: books@conkereditions.co.uk
Website: www.conkereditions.co.uk
First published by Conker Editions Ltd 2019.
Text © 2019 Derek Hammond and Gary Silke.

A CIP catalogue record for this book is available from the British Library.
13-digit ISBN: 978-1-9999008-3-0.
Design and typesetting by Gary Silke.
Printed in the UK by Mixam.

The Got, Not Got
FOOTBALL GIFT BOOK

Derek Hammond & Gary Silke

Welcome...

to the first edition of *The Got, Not Got Football Gift Book*.

As you've probably already gathered from the tempting attractions on the cover and the oddly familiar colour-coded table of contents, this is no ordinary fun-packed trawl through 20th-century football culture.

We're aiming sky high here, hoping to replicate the heart-pounding emotions once whipped up by our mums' home-shopping catalogues – those big, glossy volumes packed with endless promise. Whether your family worshipped at the altar of John Noble, Littlewoods or Grattans, the arrival of the bumper Autumn/Winter edition always sparked an unforgettable orgy of acquisitive ogling.

This book is dedicated to the small boy who would once hide away behind the sofa, crying for hours with greed, envy and lust over the contents of the Kays catalogue. The

suggests he may have a surprising amount in common with the respected, debonair football historian and collector that he grew up to be – not to mention the other 20 million overgrown kids who populate Twitter, eBay, boot sales and collector fairs, gleefully frittering away beer money on tokens of our youth.

That's right, folks. The deadly combination of football and the collector instinct – now warped to new extremes by rose-tinted nostalgia – really does bring out the worst in us.

Whenever we see a Corinthian figure or an Esso World Cup coin, or even get a whiff of a treasured Topps gum card, it can trigger a glorious flashback that comes handily bundled with all the corresponding visceral emotions.

The urge to feed the habit, completing and expanding schoolday collections, is an obsession that can all too easily turn into an

form at the back. Of course, it doesn't include *every* classic, hilarious and/or slightly rubbish item from the '60s to the '90s, but rather a judicious selection. Just like a catalogue.

In authentic style, we'll be back next time with a completely different mix of much-missed memorabilia – more classic games, kit and stickers plus whole new sections, player collections and features. Along the way, should you think of any item that you'd like to see included, please do get in touch; likewise if there's a wondrous object of desire or affection tucked away under your bed that you'd like to share with us all.

But first things first. We hope you enjoy losing yourself in this debut *Football Gift Book*. Have a great trip, whenever and wherever it might whisk you back to.

white plastic boots. The garden goal. The Action Man footballer with mod tracksuit and posing stand. They were now impossible to live without. They simply had to be possessed. And now those original Action Man club badges are worth anything up to £400 a pop. If only his mother had listened to his entirely reasonable pleas.

Sadly, modern child cruelty guidelines prevent us from identifying our frustrated infant superconsumer of the early '70s. But market research

addiction. A magical conduit back to an apparently simpler, happier golden age.

It may not be strictly possible to turn back time, but old football stuff somehow provides us with the next best thing.

The *Football Gift Book* is, in almost every respect, a fully functioning time machine as well as a real vintage catalogue. There just happens to be no order

Toys & Games Plastic Man, Take on Me

Clobber Flares and Slippers, New Boots and Panties

Programmes Two Tribes, Time of the Season

Comics & Mags Looking After Number One

Cards & Stickers I'm Waiting for the Man

Around & About Driving Away from Home

Kit Favourite Shirts, Papa's Got a Brand New Bag

Food & Drink Loaded, Sure Shot

Home & Garden The Pictures on My Wall

Tech Left to My Own Devices, 20th Century Boy

TV & Film Heroes and Villains

Tips & Training Five Man Army, New Position

Christmas The Things that Dreams Are Made of

Accessorise

Like many other junior Subbuteo devotees, the portal to my own alternative carpet-level universe was a modest entry-level set. To test the water. To see if I took to this so-called 'replica of association football.'

My folks needn't have worried unduly on that score. I'd first discovered the game round at Mitchell Stretton's house in the summer holidays – one of those unforgettable nostalgic 'JFK moments' – and approximately six seconds into my first match was already hopelessly hooked on 'reproducing all the thrills of real

football by fingertip control'. I didn't want anything in the world except that game. To own it was an absolute imperative.

And so, after long months of nagging and hinting and highly conspicuous tidying up, I finally ground them down and made a rare pilgrimage to Zodiac Toys in Leicester city centre.

My debut set was the popular Club Edition, which was as much as any average parent could afford. It contained a pitch, two goals, two teams and two balls. At last, I was in business as a player-manager-chairman.

But while I was in the toy shop, I

was also alerted to the existence of another 740 or so boxes, all in that eye-catching lime-green Subbuteo livery, and all packed with must-have accessories that promised to turn my simple baize blanket into a full-blown stadium – and then to keep on adding incrementally to the 'big-match atmosphere.'

Frustratingly, early adopter Mitchell soon had several teams to choose from when we played, as well as a scoreboard and a section

OO-heaven

Here's why you grew up with a Blue Bird Toffee addiction – and a predilection for the Sunday Express.

of terrace. But then I got a TV tower for Christmas, and all was well with the world. Although I never had (and never would) see an actual TV tower at a real football ground, the C110 remains my favourite ever gift, lovingly snapped together from flat-pack form before seven on Christmas morning. Then the

cameraman and the commentator crouching in front of his monitor really earned their corn, broadcasting for months solid, live from the living-room carpet.

My next addition was a bench set which included a manager, two trainers and John Bull lookalike Ken Baily in the bundle – a holy grail for some, especially

the left-handed rattle version!

Ken was the self-appointed England mascot who first appeared in Subbuteo form in 1967 after his decent showing at the World Cup. He came in hand-painted togs including top hat and Union Jack waistcoat – in many ways the inspiration for Gareth Southgate at the 2018 tournament.

Taking a fence:
Subbuteo moves with
the times in the troubled '80s.

Madmen

At the time, back in the '70s, I imagined the Subbuteo adverts appearing in *Shoot!* must somehow have been modelled on my own personal story. It was uncanny. 'Kid goes round to mate's house and gets the table soccer bug.' The storyline was a dead ringer, right down to the dialogue.

"I'll show you my Subbuteo – it's great!"

Except, of course, the marketing men had cunningly substituted in a different name. And so it was 'Roger' who soon mastered the famous Subbuteo, swerving his

men just like in the real game.

"Mother and father, I need to tell you about this exciting game... And floodlights! It's all so real."

You can probably guess what happened next, if only because the same plotline unfolded in your house, too. Even though, strangely, your name isn't Roger, either.

Once you'd started off down the road to Subbuteo addiction with your relatively inexpensive starter set, no birthday or Christmas could pass without a couple of items being mercifully struck off off your optimistic list of 20 or 30 most urgent immediate needs.

The absolute genius of the Subbuteo universe was that it was continually expanding. If you were lucky enough for your Auntie June to buy you a C140 Stadium Grandstand for your birthday, you couldn't help noticing how lonely it looked, sitting there on its own at the side of the pitch. And as for the fans cheering on your team, the five supporters who came along with the stand didn't add much to the legendary Subbuteo stadium atmosphere mentioned regularly on all the checklists of accessories. What you really needed was a couple more boxes

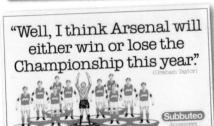

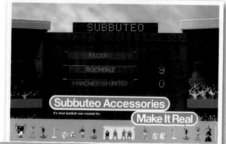

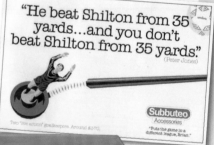

SUBBUTEO TABLE SOCCER

of fans to keep them company. And a couple more grandstands to keep *it* company, along with some terracing. Straight bits and corner bits. And some evil-looking spiked barriers to keep your unruly hordes at bay.

And you wouldn't want to be banned from the Football League because you couldn't fulfil your evening fixtures, would you? After all, what kind of a football club didn't have a ground with floodlights?

And what kind of team kept playing the same old opposition every week? You needed a decent selection of other teams to play, like the ones you'd seen in the toy shop, arrayed like little chocolates in an inviting, open box. Not just the 92 Football League clubs and the Scottish teams, mind, but yet more exotic foreign outfits kitted out in chequerboard squares, sashes and asymmetric stripes.

Choose Ards. Choose Hamilton Academicals. Choose Botafogo away. Choose real-life table-top football thrills.

figure of fun

Vivid Imaginations
▲ Soccer Super Heroes
A. David Beckham
B. Peter Schmeichel
C. Alan Shearer
D. David Seaman
E. Robbie Fowler
Ages 4 years +.
£6.49 each

It's rude to point; but David has just spotted Robbie's preposterous nose plaster.

Europa-cup
KWARTET

Rinus Israël
geboren 19 maart 1942
Libera bij Feyenoord
Rotterdam

KWARTET

Ultra Vivid Scene

They may have been too cumbersome for kids to play with, and too bulky for even the greatest collector to want the whole set, but the Vivid Imaginations series of player figures was one of the most successful of the '90s.

At over seven inches tall, you certainly got a hefty chunk of plastic for your £6.49, and heroes of the era still pop up regularly on fans' sideboards.

The figurines' ultimate irony was that they incorporated pleasing likenesses of the players, so you didn't need a vivid imagination at all to tell your Gazza from your Alan Shearer.

It's Dutch for 'Quartet', Yeah?

While British kids didn't get to join the hot Top Trumps cult until 1978, Kwartet cards were popular in the Netherlands even in the '60s. Featuring footballers, cars, cats and so on, the game's simple object was to collect up four-card subsets, like in Happy Families.

One of the most sought-after packs, then and now, commemorated the 1970 European Cup, which saw Feyenoord beat Celtic in the final. Today even single

Just look at the microscopic brushwork on that Wrexham badge.

Painter Man

Back in the '60s and '70s Airfix was mostly concerned with giving schoolkids the means to recreate 1/32- and 00-scale versions of World War II, still fresh in grown-

cards can change hands for over a fiver, despite (or perhaps partly because of) the manufacturer's *laissez-faire* attitude to naming the then giants of British football.

ups' memories and central to our culture. But away from the miniature Afrika Korps invasions and Lancaster bomber kits, they also produced Airfix Footballers.

It wasn't immediately obvious as a child what to do with your little plastic players, which arrived quite naked in their box, the colour of chewed lemon Refreshers. The idea was to paint them up using a brush with no more than three

hairs and tiny pots of Humbrol paint, a task better suited to much older boys.

The advent of eBay and the football nostalgia movement saw many of them eventually decked out in classic kits. Blessed with a steady hand, I completed several commissions before breaking a finger at five-a-side. The Plymouth Argyle set now lives happily on the US West Coast.

Striking Gold

For anyone like us, who only ever played Striker with the random teams provided in the standard, original game, it's quite sickening (in the best possible way) to discover the glories of James Hills' rare and enviable team sets.

"In 1977 Palitoy introduced their Super Striker range," James takes up the story, "which featured a real Astroturf Wembley pitch and built-in pitch barrier. No more lost hours trying to erect the old tape barrier around the pitch! And best of all were the new teams. The All-star range had modern-looking kits such as Man United and Newcastle as well as ones that looked like Ipswich/Everton, Palace, Middlesbrough, Leeds away, Birmingham and Coventry away. No longer did you have to paint your Parker teams to create your favourite sides. There were even left- and right-footed players so you could play the ball down the line against the barrier.

"I took on a paper round, washing cars, walking dogs. I'd do anything to get the money to go down to the local toy shop to get my next team. Then things

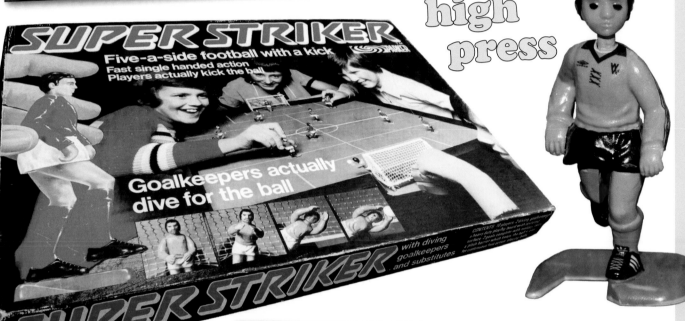

moved on to another level when actual teams came out. Liverpool, Everton, Man City, Spurs, Arsenal, Forest, Villa and Leeds teams meant yet more jobs to fund yet more toy shop trips. Now you could play out a whole league fixture list, with results and up-to-date tables to be added to your school exercise book after each round of games.

"Those new team sets with the colourful rosettes were the hottest thing in the school playground. Until, one week, I turned the page in the latest copy of *Shoot!* and found a full-page advert for the new international teams!"

Our thanks go out to James for his memories, his team sets and wonderful custom-painted sets.

What a time to discover we had a deprived childhood.

The Watford striker suffered a career-threatening pulled neck when one young player attempted a backheel.

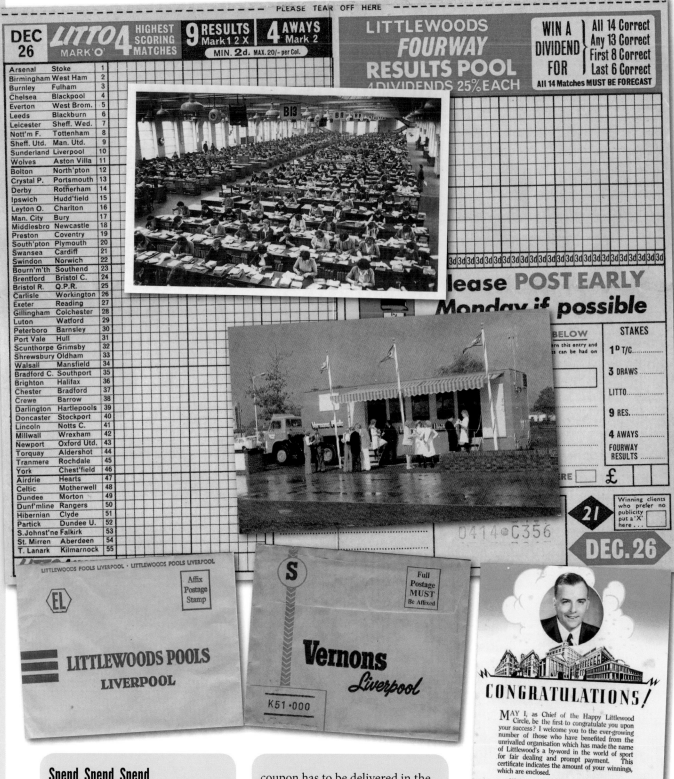

DEC 26	**LITTO4** MARK 'O'	**HIGHEST SCORING 4 MATCHES**

9 RESULTS Mark 1 2 X · MIN. **2d.** MAX. 20/- per Col.

4 AWAYS Mark 2

LITTLEWOODS FOURWAY RESULTS POOL 4 DIVIDENDS 25% EACH

WIN A DIVIDEND FOR
- All 14 Correct
- Any 13 Correct
- First 8 Correct
- Last 6 Correct

All 14 Matches MUST be FORECAST

Arsenal	Stoke	1
Birmingham	West Ham	2
Burnley	Fulham	3
Chelsea	Blackpool	4
Everton	West Brom.	5
Leeds	Blackburn	6
Leicester	Sheff. Wed.	7
Nott'm F.	Tottenham	8
Sheff. Utd.	Man. Utd.	9
Sunderland	Liverpool	10
Wolves	Aston Villa	11
Bolton	North'pton	12
Crystal P.	Portsmouth	13
Derby	Rotherham	14
Ipswich	Hudd'field	15
Leyton O.	Charlton	16
Man. City	Bury	17
Middlesbro	Newcastle	18
Preston	Coventry	19
South'pton	Plymouth	20
Swansea	Cardiff	21
Swindon	Norwich	22
Bourn'm'th	Southend	23
Brentford	Bristol C.	24
Bristol R.	Q.P.R.	25
Carlisle	Workington	26
Exeter	Reading	27
Gillingham	Colchester	28
Luton	Watford	29
Peterboro	Barnsley	30
Port Vale	Hull	31
Scunthorpe	Grimsby	32
Shrewsbury	Oldham	33
Walsall	Mansfield	34
Bradford C.	Southport	35
Brighton	Halifax	36
Chester	Bradford	37
Crewe	Barrow	38
Darlington	Hartlepools	39
Doncaster	Stockport	40
Lincoln	Notts C.	41
Millwall	Wrexham	42
Newport	Oxford Utd.	43
Torquay	Aldershot	44
Tranmere	Rochdale	45
York	Chest'field	46
Airdrie	Hearts	47
Celtic	Motherwell	48
Dundee	Morton	49
Dunf'mline	Rangers	50
Hibernian	Clyde	51
Partick	Dundee U.	52
S.Johnst'ne	Falkirk	53
St. Mirren	Aberdeen	54
T. Lanark	Kilmarnock	55

lease **POST EARLY** Monday if possible

3d 3d 3d 3d 3d 3d 3d 3d 3d 3d 3d 3d 3d 3d 3d 3d 3d 3d 3d 3d 3d 3d

STAKES	
1ᴰ T/C	
3 DRAWS	
LITTO	
9 RES.	
4 AWAYS	
FOURWAY RESULTS	

£

Winning clients who prefer no publicity put a 'X' here . . .

21

0414•C356

DEC. 26

Spend, Spend, Spend

Happy Christmas! At least, that was the idea when we were planning to reproduce a complete original football pools coupon, ready for you to clip and send in to those nice people at Littlewoods/Zetters/Vernons.

All you had to do was look up the results for Boxing Day 1964, fill in your confident predictions for the Treble Chance, and await the 'Congratulations!' letter landing on your doormat. There's nothing in the rules to say your coupon has to be delivered in the correct decade, or even century. Which might be one reason why the pools companies aren't doing quite as well as back in the day.

Coh, there was a time when almost every family had a go at picking eight draws. Vernon's vast Mobile Information Units were a welcome sight, gaily blocking city streets. And thousands of Scouse women were employed checking for rows of lucky Xs in the cavernous main hall at the Art Deco Littlewoods Building.

The timeless dream of fame and fortune is now set for a fresh boost at the beautiful Littlewoods site, which is currently being converted into a major film studios, opening in 2021 and already known as 'The Hollywood of the North'.

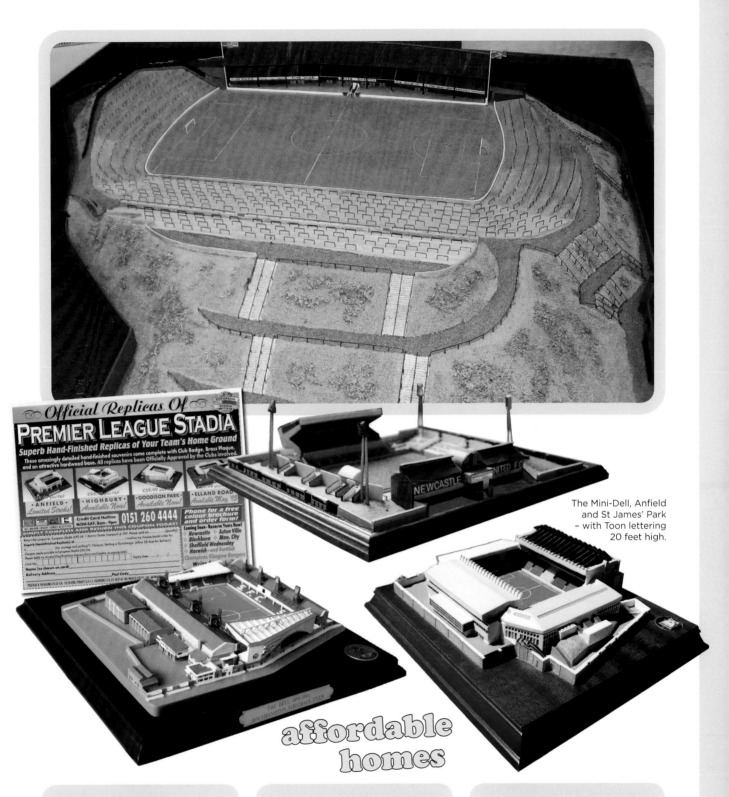

The Mini-Dell, Anfield and St James' Park – with Toon lettering 20 feet high.

affordable homes

A Stadium of One's Own

It's a childhood dream for many of us fans – to win the pools or the National Lottery and so get to own our very own football club.

Heck, if characters like Mike Ashley can grab themselves a whole Premier League club to toy with, the very least you should be aiming for is to own the stadium you've trooped to loyally year after year ever since you were a nipper.

The home where your heart is. However, should neither outrageous fortune nor the Russian Mafia ever smile your way, a stadium model is a decent fallback. An ideal centrepiece for the family breakfast table, and a canny conversation starter for when your friends are round.

Costing £44.99 a shot at '90s prices, these mini-ancestral stamping grounds were a bit of a

dear do; but they did stand the test when you got down on your hands and knees and pretended to be there, once you'd had a sherbet.

Best of all are the architectural models of old sporting venues built with such love and detail by Aly at Craigleith Art & Design. This terrific '50s Easter Road may not be every Hibs fan's partner's dream; but how cool to have an actual hilltop fort in your den.

19

LIVERPOOL 3 LEICESTER CITY 1.

7 F.A. Cup semi-final replay, Villa Park, 1973-74 season.

This goal will live with me forever because it was technically perfect. I began my run inside the Leicester half and, unusually for me, struck from 25 yards. The ball soared above the level of the crossbar to clear model goalkeeper Peter Shilton then "dip" sweetly into the top corner.

a good rub-down

User warning: staring for too long at this Letraset scene may cause dizziness.

It's the Amazing Football Ace with a Plunger Imbedded in His Bottom.

Transfer Market

Imagine my unbridled joy when I finally laid hands on the Kevin Keegan Letraset pack No.7 that featured Leicester City. Faced with the eternal tough choice of every true collector – whether to hoard it forever in pristine mint condition – I tore it open excitedly and got my best HB pencil out.

Simply by scribbling on the greaseproof paper backing, I could have relived the 1974 FA Cup semi-final replay against Liverpool at Villa Park. However, Kevvy Keegle had since wound me up with his boasting: "The goal will live with me forever because it was technically perfect..." so I decided to rewrite history. In my alternate Letraset timeline he sees his 'perfect' shot saved by Shilts, who has perfected a new upside-down save which he calls 'The Bat'. Graham Cross is astounded, while Brian Hall is so confused he bashes his coccyx on the goalpost and has to be stretchered off.

Without him, City overrun the Reds' midfield, win the game 5-2 and beat Newcastle in the final.

Up yours, Keegle.

Goalgetter by Name

The action-figure gurus at Mego designed Steve Goalgetter in direct response to kids' criticisms of Action Man Footballer. Steve had bendy knees; he didn't just stand in a frame but could actually shoot thanks to a syringe in his rear end, and he came complete with cut-out defenders and a goal. But somehow he just never caught on.

men of action

Historical Hornets: Action Men model some surprising Watford kits.

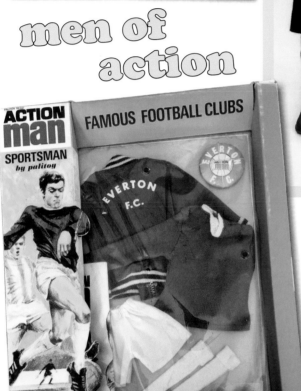

ACTION man
SPORTSMAN
by palitoy

FAMOUS FOOTBALL CLUBS

EVERTON F.C.

EVERTON

CONTENTS
- tracksuit top
- shirt and numbers
- shorts
- socks
- boots
- ball
- lapel badge
- club history leaflet

Collect these Stars towards your free Action Man gifts ★ ★ ★

Roving Eyes and Gripping Hands

Despite the limitations of playing with Action Man Footballer, the soldier-*cum*-striker proved to have real staying power. We put this down to the indefinable poise of the Palitoy favourite, the *je ne sais quoi* that inspired mums to create chunky-knit kits for him in the thrifty '70s, and collectors to pay ever-spiralling prices for his original club kits.

You may think it ridiculous that anyone would pay £800 for a miniature Everton kit, but it's a true measure of AM's status as a childhood icon. Like Alan Ball or Pat Nevin. Only even smaller.

Let's compare and contrast the 12-inch action-figure extension of the popular Corinthians range of models in the '90s. Yes, Power Play figures had kicking power. The goalies' spring-loaded reflexes were as snappy as a mousetrap. And then there was the untold benefit of interchangeable heads.

But poise? Not really. A Power Play game could take on the rather eerie atmosphere of a crime scene.

puzzled?

Pick Up the Pieces

They used to be a rainy-day pastime foisted on the young as a last resort by unusually cruel or patient parents. Who doesn't recall the dread moment on Christmas Day when you tentatively picked up the shallow oblong prezzie from Auntie Kath, dreading the familiar shaky sound of a jigsaw puzzle secreted inside? Give us a selection box every time, Auntie.

Strangely, things have now gone full circle, and the market for jigsaws chiefly comprises octagenarian parents and stressed-out executive types. There's no time in the modern world for piecing together a portrait of Martin Peters that has been shattered into 500 pieces.

And yet, as usual, there's an exception to the rule. Football collectors can't get enough of vintage jigsaws, and the market price of the least sexy soccer spin-off is rising fast.

Whether an action shot, a portrait or teamgroup, a Coffer Sports classic or an '80s jobbie that came in a tube like Pringles, the humble football jigsaw is now well worth picking up for pennies at any car boot sale.

The nightmare is having to do the puzzle to prove that it's complete. Especially when it's not.

Get happy: Gazza's unique grin captured perfectly by the Corinthian sculptor.

Ace of base: Promotional figures in beer and biscuit company livery.

Corinthian Spirit

Do you remember that particular feeling of stumping up £1.99 for a Corinthians Pro Stars 'secret sachet' not knowing who you were going to get? It could be one of your club's stars, an obscurity or even a player you struggled to recognise – good, bad or ugly.

The figure of Gazza released in series 3, sporting the Italia 90 strip, was a great sculpt. Likewise that of West Ham's feisty full-back Julian Dicks. But, unfortunately for Lee Bowyer, whoever sculpted his figure must have had an off day. Lee was only 20 when this came out, not 60!

It wasn't just fans who had opinions on the likenesses: "I was comfortable with mine," commented Man United's Brian McClair, "however, I remember Pally hating his!"

Corinthians went on to enjoy a rollercoaster history and to spawn a whole collector culture, from devoted conventions to special promotions, releasing figures in conjunction with Jaffa Cakes, Tiger Beer, MOTD and Pepsi. One of the rarest figures you'll ever find is the WHSmith release of Gianluca Vialli in Chelsea's all-yellow away kit, only available from stores along with the purchase of a VHS season review.

All of these items were kindly supplied by Michael Kennard, aka @CorinthianHead on Twitter, the go-to guy on the subject. His page covers the whole history of the little bigheads alongside player chat, unreleased figures, custom repainters and much more.

Arsenal

Baggy Trousers

Can it really be 29 years ago when Lee Dixon modelled this smashing JVC running vest in the Gunners' annual pre-season clobber catalogue?

Back in 1990,

deep in the era of baggy fashion, it's clear that Hammer pants were also state of art, modelled manfully along with a controversial line in quartered rugby tops by 'Rocky' Rocastle and Brian Marwood. But when it came to carrying off the Adidas club shellsuit – or the League championship, with his unforgettable last-minute clincher, just weeks before this shoot – there was no one quite like Michael Thomas.

Aston Villa

We Are the Champions

We hope you appreciate the engineering quality in this historic chunk of Villa motorabilia. For full effect, it really needs to be viewed in graceful motion in the rear windscreen of a classic '80s motor – a locally made Rover 3500, perhaps, like John Steed's? – where the fine-tooled sprung steel and double sucker action really come into their own.

The ball floats slowly, invitingly, time and time again in front of our title winner (surely modelled on then recently departed midfielder, John Gregory?), so he gets endless chances to volley the ball home and confirm the club's Division One triumph. Europe, here Villa come!

Birmingham City

The Paintbox Kit

The early '90s saw a period of instability at St Andrew's. But despite player unrest and the revolving-door managerial policy of the owners, the Kumar brothers, Blues did win the Leyland DAF Trophy in 1991 and promotion back to the second tier in '92.

Then the infamous 'Paintbox' kit was debuted, boasting a stylistic flair typical of the owners' Mark One stores. Controversially, it also featured a traditional club badge recoloured to echo the Indian flag, as well as orange and green sock tops. When the collapse of the Kumars' bank unluckily put the club in receivership, the takeover by jazz-mag baron David Sullivan was seen as a mixed blessing – but the axing of the unpopular kit, mid season, was at least one instant positive.

Blackburn Rovers

Spending Small

Nowadays, it seems faintly ridiculous to accuse Rovers chairman Jack Walker of having 'bought' the Premier League when his previously unfashionable club raced away to the third ever iteration of the competition in 1995. First, Jack made Alan Shearer the most expensive player in English football (£3.5 million from Southampton) then added Chris Sutton (£4.5 million from Norwich), spending a total of just £27 million on his championship squad.

Just as Walker had assembled his victorious team, the arrival of Corinthians All Stars in 1995 enabled you to do exactly the same, at only a fraction of the outlay. (About 27 per cent, adjusting for overinflated 2019 PL prices.)

Blackpool

Mixed Grille

If you're lucky enough to own a car from a time when not all motors looked exactly alike, then you'll need one of these beauties bolted to your bumper as the final word in effortless cool.

That said, cars that didn't all look the same did tend to have something else in common.

Breaking down. So what better to speed you on your way to Bloomfield Road than this vintage *dual-purpose* grille badge.

Not only does it flag you up as a proud Tangerine. A Seasider with style. It also puts in a good word with Him Upstairs to ensure that you and your whip arrive in one piece: verily, 'Behold St Christopher, and go your way in safety'.

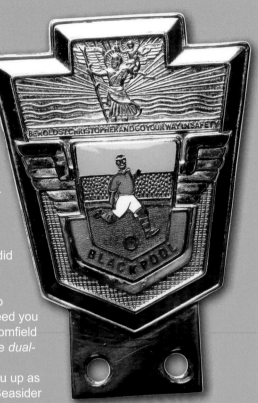

And should you merely be the owner of a ten-a-penny Astra/Metro/Polo/Megane/Focus, it'll help identify which one is your boring silver jalopy in the car park.

Bournemouth

Ted Talks

If you're looking for advice on football shorts, why not pop along to Ted MacDougall Sports in Bournemouth?

The Cherries' star will be right there behind the counter, eager to dish out his expert views on all kinds of shorts – whether you want them with drawstrings, German designed or in just the same style sported by AFCB's finest.

You'll probably end up so chuffed with your new shorts, you won't want to ruin the look with other less stylish kit.

Be like Ted. Just say no to shirts.

A short cut to a new look!

The "Cherries" new look shorts – the first team in the country to sport them. Styled and manufactured in West Germany by "Allround." Come along to Ted's new Sports Store and see for yourself his line up of sports equipment. New look shorts, football boots, squash rackets, tennis rackets, you name it and more than likely Ted's got it ! Just advice you want ? Then come along – you'll be more than welcome.

TED MacDOUGALL SPORTS LTD
712a Christchurch Road, Boscombe, Bournemouth. Telephone 37455
Gannett Sportswear Ltd, Poole – U.K. distributors for Allround Sports, West Germany's top manufacturer of Action Sportswear

Allround

Brighton & Hove Albion

Up the Aquatic Mammals

There was a stampede for trendy new club nicknames in the '70s, as marketing became more prevalent in the game. Thence Filberts became Foxes, Glaziers Eagles and Biscuitmen the Royals...

What Brighton – plain old

'Albion' to their mates – really needed was an animal alter-ego, so that the mascot could dress up as a big furry...

yes, a dolphin would do just fine.

However, the club reckoned without the grass-roots influence of thousands of fans chanting "Seagulls, Seagulls" in response to their Palace rivals' "Eagles, Eagles." And so dolphin chic proved short lived.

Bristol City

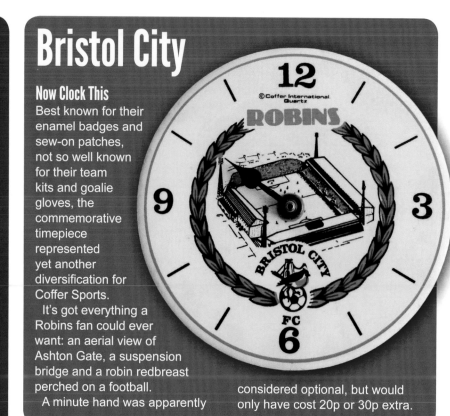

Now Clock This

Best known for their enamel badges and sew-on patches, not so well known for their team kits and goalie gloves, the commemorative timepiece represented yet another diversification for Coffer Sports.

It's got everything a Robins fan could ever want: an aerial view of Ashton Gate, a suspension bridge and a robin redbreast perched on a football.

A minute hand was apparently considered optional, but would only have cost 20p or 30p extra.

Bristol Rovers

How to Do Quarters

Here's young Patrick Morgan back in 1975, modelling a textbook Pirates shirt from the time. It's a classic in fine traditional quartered style.

Call us sticklers (or downright philistines) but there's one more detail that could have added an extra fillip, and that's the reverse-colour collar band the club used to wear right up until the '50s – blue on the white side and vice-versa. Still, a classic.

Moving on swiftly more than two decades to the 1996/97 season, here's the shirt that stands as a perfect example of how *not* to do quarters.

Adopted at the time that Rovers finally moved back to Bristol from their long exile in Bath, the shirt known locally as the 'Tesco bag' was a bogey up the nose of a season of celebration.

clobber

NEW GEORGIE BEST Strikers

ALL ACTION SHOES– FOR ALL ACTION BOYS

GUARANTEED 6 MONTHS NORMAL WEAR

Wear your Best shoes for school—Play out in them.
New Georgie Best Strikers are real boys' shoes.
Strong and tough like the people who wear them.
With a terrific Georgie Best action footballer sole
that leaves super tracks wherever you go.
When they're dirty just wash 'em—and they'll look
like new.
Tell your Mum, tell your friends about Georgie Best
Strikers—the Best shoes for you!

From all good shoe shops

FREE with every pair this terrific GEORGIE BEST COLOUR POSTER with 10 great on the Ball soccer tips. Only with Georgie Best Strikers.

STYLO Matchmakers

FROM ONLY **£1·99**

Products of Stylo Matchmakers International Ltd. Matchmaker House Clayton Wood Bank Leeds LS16 6RJ

September 4, 1971   **GOAL**   **25**

World Cup 1966
THE OFFICIAL TIE IN
TRICEL®
by the makers of the famous
TRICELUX®
TIE

Available from all leading outfitters, sports suppliers and stores.

FAVOURITE TIES LTD
Block C, 28 Oxford Street, Manchester 1. Tel: CENtral 7651.

Georgie Best Strikers

I still remember the shock of discovering leopard tracks in the mud out by the mobile classrooms at junior school. I wasn't alarmed. Each big cat print was perfectly centred in the outline of a size 4 boy's school shoe. Just jealous.

I'd seen the comic ads for Clark's Commandos, had heard word of kids with compasses hidden in their insoles, and had searched for secret compartments in my own new school shoes, alas in vain.

Given that football trumps any dumb animal by a factor of ten, I struggle to guess how I would have reacted to finding *Georgie Best* tracks in the mud on the way down to the playground. Wow, just imagine the long-haired bad boy

of Manchester United staggering past the kitchens, stalking any unsuspecting Miss Worlds grazing on the football field – that would have been utterly mind-blowing.

Only today does the euphemism 'wipe-clean' give me a sweet pang of *schadenfreude* at the expense of the lucky Stylo kids, learning soccer tips from Georgie's poster.

Yes, the shoes were plastic. But I still yearn for a pair, and the chance to leave a trail of awed squeals in my muddy wake.

Mackay's Ties

When Cloughie made the inspired move of signing the veteran Dave Mackay from Spurs, he converted the triple FA Cup-winning skipper into a sweeper. Derby promptly

won promotion from Division Two, and Mackay was named joint FWA Footballer of the Year.

Clough put the great Scottish leader on £16,000 a year, more than Best or Greaves, Moore or Law. And there were other non-contract stipulations to be cleared up before Mackay would sign on the dotted line – such as a special dispensation to enjoy a sherbet on Monday through Thursday nights... and Cloughie moving training to Tuesdays so that Dave could have Sundays and Mondays off, to look after his Mackay's Ties business down in London.

dress like a star

Managers Coat Sizes: M/L/XL £69.99

Clobber Maketh the Man

There can be no greater compliment than basing your own personal style on that of a hero, hoping that some of their charm or skill will rub off like magic dust.

1 – In truth, your chances of turning into a lightning-fast goal poacher may be slim, but we'd still recommend getting Gary Lineker's mum to iron your jeans.

2 – And look at the effect Peter Shilton's razor-creased slacks have on his bevy of admirers in Stoke.

3 – Buy a patterned V-neck and you'll soon be stroking the ball around the park like Glenn Hoddle – or, at least, Paul Miller.

4 –Behind every successful manager there's the back of a big coat. No matter if it looks too long, has a Huddersfield Town logo and costs £70, invest now and you'll soon be pacing the technical area with top boss Neil Warnock.

5 – Or go the whole hog and blow an extra £29 on George Graham conversation-starter cuffs.

Even in the loved-up, easy-grooving '60s, it was inadvisable to shout at the back of a copper's head.

The Kop Catwalk

Football fans were once again in the news when Leicester City hosted Liverpool at Filbert Street on 7 October 1967. Seventy innocent bystanders were caught up in the excitement – not of a minor scuffle, you understand, but of an impromptu fashion parade.

Captured by our opportunistic snapper like flies in aspic, they now provide us with a rare and fascinating glimpse of what fans were wearing to the match back in the Swinging '60s.

1 – An interesting variation on the home-made bar scarf and bobble-hat look. Look, no bobble.

2 – When was the last time you saw a Bobby at a football match or on the beat wearing a proper helmet? And what about a pair of white gloves as an ultimate touch of old-school cop class?

3 – Wouldn't it be amazing if we could somehow find this fan and watch his Super-8 film of the match, including a reverse view of these cops on the Pop Side and the photographer up on the cinder track, pitchside?

4 – It's an outfit of two halves, Brian. Scuffed shoes, jeans and a lived-in cardigan with those brown buttons that looked a bit like little leather footballs. But still toting a necktie.

5 – Enter Mr Cool. That hair is seriously long for 1967, but the wraparound shades and medallion mark out this chap as a groover of the highest order. He's lucky the copper didn't arrest him on sight for ungentlemanly conduct, or for a breach of the neckwear by-laws.

6 – Believe it or not, this was a thing. Wearing a miner's helmet or builder's hard hat to the match. No, really. This guy wasn't alone.

7 – Nice rosette let down by a scruffy loose tie. Poor show.

8 – Mod sports shirt buttoned up to the neck, tight jean jacket, red-and-white trilby and home-made Liverpool scarf. Fresh out of The Cavern, daddy-o.

9 – A sure sign that this was the good old days: kids sitting on the wall down the front! Got to love this little chap's school cap, smart white socks and mini version of his dad's check overcoat.

31

scarf ACE!

Neck- and Wristwear Dept.

Have you ever worn a garment other than a football scarf that features *tassles*? Just asking, like.

In the beginning was the woollen bar scarf, home-knitted by your mum or gran. It wasn't just about their nurturing urge to keep your neck cosy in winter. Before the football merch explosion of the late '60s, it was nigh on impossible to buy a scarf in club colours, let alone adorned with your team's name. That's where darning wool came in, and an extra request for mum, ideally at the rate of one big capital letter per stripe.

Next came the 'silk' scarf, mostly used to keep your wrist warm while goading oppo fans. Notice those inverted commas around 'silk'. Occasionally you might find a classy, crushably soft scarf that arguably had silky qualities, but mostly they were stubbornly stiff, 2-D nylon, better suited to the wall than the wardrobe.

The greatest technological leap in neck- and wristwear came in the '70s with a process that enabled colour printing on nylon scarves. Woo-hoo. It's just a shame that the same trick worked on the next generation of *faux*-wool fanwear, with its unfortunate tendency toward flowery typefaces.

Collector's item: The last time Manchester City would win a major trophy for 35 years.

pack up your troubles...

School: Bags of Fun

For a big plastic receptacle, the humble school bag can hold an unusual power over your heartstrings – along with its everyday contents, of course.

One geography book, covered in left-over wallpaper. One chemistry textbook. Your rough book, so called because of the cheap texture of the paper. Your packed lunch: Monster Munch, jam sandwich and a banana. Helix trigonometry set. Tennis ball for lunchtime football game. Large bundle of Panini '79 harnessed by a stout laggy band.

Out of all the schoolday fads and accessories that football fans seek to claw back into their possession, the Adidas-style holdall, the over-the-shoulder sports bag and duffle bag offer the best excuses. They actually have a use, as well as collector value. And you can always tell your wife it's something to do with Northern Soul.

double knitting

On Me 'Ead!

It's a bloody good job that bobble hats exist. Even now we're long past the era when the stripy woolly hat pulled down over the ears worked as shorthand for a football fan in popular culture – in TV comedy sketches, on postcards – they're still vital to our way of life.

Why? Because if it wasn't for the bobble hat, there'd be no such thing as the pom-pom. And it's pretty much impossible to imagine a civilised society where small children don't have to face the rite of passage involving two circles of cardboard, a ball of wool and a drizzly Sunday afternoon with nothing better to do.

Here's a knitting pattern with origins north of the border, where bobble hats are still commonly required all year round, never mind your southern softie so-called winters. It's clear how happy the Scottish fans are to have helped their nannas create their bobbles. Although the Motherwell family, it must be said, does seem to have been rather short-changed.

Each to his/her own opinion; but surely even a disappointing pom-pom must beat a corporate nylon Bob Dylan or Chairman Mao?

titfers!

34

1966 mascot, World Cup Willie, spawned 1000 souvenirs and the first ever World Cup song, by Lonnie Donegan.

belt & braces

Blinging It

Although Coffer Sports has always been synonymous with football bling of the very highest order, a long-lost '70s mail-order catalogue recently reminded us exactly why the Northampton company remains one of the most collectable manufacturers of all kinds of vintage fan memorabilia.

Yes, Coffer famously produced thousands of enamel badges, pendants, necklaces and rings. But just as vital were the hats, mugs, iron-on transfers, patches, pennants, kits, flags, keyrings, scarves, penknives, bags and belts. Not just football. Pop stars, too!

If only it were possible to send back in time a £3.00 postal order

to your junior self – enough to buy about half of the goodies in the catalogue. Oh, for a football flask and a pair of groundbreaking Coffer goalie gloves.

Half-mast Trouser Dept.

What a decision for any true connoisseur of vintage style to have to make. What would you go for? A pair of World Cup Willie braces, direct from the 1966 World

Cup finals? Or a Trebor star-studded pop or soccer belt?

Genuine Willie suspenders are rare, pricy and going up all the time. But a Trebor belt would give you the added chance to express yourself. It isn't everyone who sports a Jim McCalliog/David Bowie belt one day, and a Tommy Smith/Dave Hill combo the next.

At the *Got, Not Got Football Gift Book* we're all about choice.

PS I Love You

It's the age-old question. How to let everybody else know that you like really cool stuff?

Today, practically everybody has got a full sleeve of tattoos or a message on their back for special friends. But back in the Golden Age of Inking a tat meant you were part of an exclusive scene – most likely a pirate or a lady in a circus sideshow.

Badges were always the most popular way to display our personal enthusiasms. They represented a sensible strategy, too, meaning you'd never need to undergo seven hours of painful laser surgery to reclaim your thigh, several decades after eventually weaning yourself off Daphne out of *Neighbours*.

True, your unrequited love for a football team is meant to last for life; but getting a tattoo of the badge can create more problems than it solves. Firstly, if you go for a giant city coat-of-arms that covers your whole back, you need to take off your shirt in order to show off the object of your faith. Secondly, for fans of a certain vintage, a huge Smiley icon or cartoon peacock inked across your forehead might be open to mistaken interpretation.

The age-old answer is a Coffer enamel badge pinned discreetly to your lapel.

They often come bundled with a winning pun. 'Everton Gotta Lottle Bottle', with a picture of a pinta. 'West Ham Turn Me On', complete with female bottom in suspenders. Great fun. Practical, too, should the joke start to wear thin after 40 years. Or, God forbid, if fickle fashions were to change.

Plymouth's unique shirt with the green-and-black band and Mayflower crest was a nailed-on '60s classic.

Look Proper Posh with TOFFS

Looking back on a rose-tinted past has become ever more complicated since the 1970s, when clubs started bringing out official replica football shirts to satisfy fans' demands.

Coh, do you remember those slower, simpler times when the site of your new superstadium was all fields, and the only shirts you could buy were the current designs of the day?

The first chance we got to buy a replica shirt from a previous age came in the '90s, with the rise of the The Old Fashioned Football Shirt (TOFFS – geddit?) dynasty.

Now it was possible not only to go to the pub with 'SHEARER 9' across your back, but also in '70s style like Malcolm Macdonald or in 'Wor Jackie' Milburn's button-up stripes.

TOFFS shirts were solid quality and strangely influential. Not long after they brought out an 1878 Newton Heath shirt with lace-up collar, Ryan Giggs was wearing one out on the pitch, as clubs first joined in the idea of cashing in on their kit history.

Today TOFFS puts us in a nostalgia loop, looking back at a kit manufacturer that popularised looking back. Confusing times.

up for the cup

A rosette for the discerning Spurs fan who only really wanted Martin Peters to win.

Do Us a Favour

Although the modern-day demise of the FA Cup is exaggerated, it's still easy to lose sight of the pure sporting excitement that every round of the competition used to whip up in the not-so-distant past.

Nowadays, as ever, peaks of fan enthusiasm are encountered when the non-League minnows first get their chance to get one over on the basking sharks of the third and fourth tier, in the third round of the Cup. That's when local TV cameras cluster in the hope of witnessing a giant killing, the promise of which for many decades provided the natural habitat of the big-match rosette – now sadly extinct.

In these times of weakened Cup squads, wearing a favour in club colours may seem old-fashioned to fans of the Premier League's multinational corporations; but in any heroic battle against the odds rosettes, bobble hats and partisan scarves surely remain the best way to show your support. A lot better, in any case, than patronising a bigger club by wearing an evil half-and-half scarf, or painting your kid's face bright blue.

Does no one else miss the illegal, unlicensed rosette seller outside the buzzing ground; the football family bonded by coloured ribbons in an act of defiance? Let's bring back the rosette.

Gola

LIVERPOOL FOOTBALL CLUB

The PE Years: when a pair of trainers meant you were probably Jonah Barrington.

Awaydays
KEVIN SAMPSON

adidas
ORIGINAL

top pumps

Trainerspotting

In the olden days, when professional football was little more than PE played out in front of a crowd, training shoes did exactly what it said on the box. They were chiefly worn for jogging around the pitch or kicking footballs through tyres suspended from the crossbar. And, oh yes. They could also be worn for playing lesser sports, such as squash or tennis.

Small children might legitimately wear trainers, plimsolls or baseball boots for PE lessons or for playing out in the school holidays, but any grown-up sporting training shoes in the pub would be assumed to be an amateur boxer ducking out of his roadwork.

Popular culture has a lot to answer for. In the '70s, trainers became trendy. By the '80s, they had become the footwear of choice for the majority of fans at any match. As a result manufacturers began to take the piss. Branded trainers became wildly expensive, objects of fetishistic pride for hooligans dressed in their dads' casual knitwear and golf slacks.

In the '90s, football clubs sidled coolly into the marketplace. After all, who *didn't* want a pair of multi-coloured foam-and-plastic bootees with a picture of a generic player on the sole? We might even get to perform the Trainer Sutra like Leicester's lucky Lee Philpott.

39

MAGPIE

OFFICIAL MATCH-DAY MAGAZINE   PRICE 35p

WHAT'S GOING ON ON DECEMBER 4th ?
WRANGLER THAT'S WHAT'S GOING ON

FOOTBALL LEAGUE, DIVISION ONE
Notts County v Nottingham Forest
Saturday, 4th December, 1982, kick-off 3 p.m.

Wrangler
SPONSORED MATCH

ROVERS *Review*

The Official Programme of
Tranmere Rovers Football Club
Season 1983-84   25p

It was "a Happy Birthday" for Dave Philpotts

ASSOCIATE MEMBERS CUP - NORTHERN AREA SEMI-FINAL
SEASON 1983 - 84
TUESDAY 17th APRIL 1984 KICK OFF 7.30 p.m
● MATCH SPONSORS - PEERS BONNAR & CO. ●
TRANMERE ROVERS v BURNLEY
ALL PAY. Season tickets and V.P. Lounge tickets cannot be used for
this game. (Competition Rule 16.)

.. 1472 IS YOUR FREE DRAW N..

❼

🎶 HUGH FOULERTON CUTLERY

BLUESNEWS

TODAY LEAGUE DIVISION TWO—SEASON 1986-87   OFFICIAL PROGRAMME—PRICE 60p

BIRMINGHAM CITY
v
READING

★ *Birmingham City Shirt Sponsors...*
CO-OP MILK

Football League, Division 3.   Kick-off 7.30 p.m.
MONDAY, 6th MARCH 1978
WREXHAM v. TRANMERE ROVERS
Official Programme — 15p.

❽

W R E X H A M

ALBION ROVERS v. STENHOUSEMUIR

❺

Match Programme 10p.

covered in glory

THE DON

ABERDEEN v ST MIRREN
SATURDAY 8th OCTOBER 1983
PREMIER DIVISION FOOTBALL
OFFICIAL MATCHDAY MAGAZINE 40p

PROFILE ON
NEALE COOPER

THE ROBIN

16 PAGE
SPECIAL ISSUE
PRICE 30p

LEAGUE DIVISION ONE
BRISTOL CITY v EVERTON
OFFICIAL MATCHDAY
PROGRAMME PRICE 30p

EVERTON

LEAGUE DIVISION ONE   SATURDAY 26th MARCH 1977   PROGRAMME 15p

"Joining Everton
took my breath away
for a week or so.." says
physiotherapist Jim
McGregor in today's
'Goodison Gallery'
feature.

EVERTON v TOTTENHAM H.

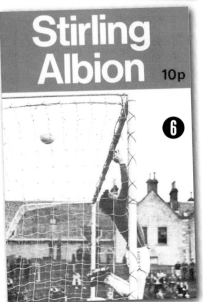

Stirling Albion 10p

❻

The Sky Strikers World Cup

It was one of the greatest events of 2018, a World Cup that would be remembered for all the right reasons by football fans around the globe.

Trading under the username of @TheSkyStrikers, Australian ex-pat Miles McLagan has made a huge number of friends on social media by selflessly loading online complete scans of his vast collection of vintage football programmes. What's more, he highlights all the best bits along the way, offering a unique patchwork insight into the

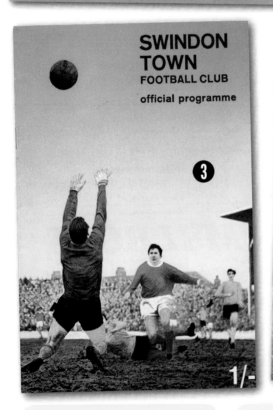

humdrum world of British football in the late 20th century.

It was a natural next step to set his most popular posts head to head, round after round, to discover the vintage programme World Cup winner by way of popular vote. Many can now boast near-legendary status:

8 – The sheep in the crowd at the Racecourse Ground was unlucky not to progress beyond the round of 16.

7 – It's the stripper in the Tranmere Rovers dressing room.

6 – The haunting, evocative Stirling Albion cover that became known as 'Crowd'.

5 – A vivid collage from Albion Rovers. Can you spot what's real and what's been drawn on?

Taking their place in the stellar battles of the quarter-finals were:

4 – Some big characters up an alley outside Molineux in 1977.

3 – The Swindon striker who

looks huge because of a primitive colour printing process.

2 – The documentary classic that became known as 'Dons Wean'.

1 – And the worthy winner, the 1979 Boro cover starring an infamous goalie only too chuffed to see the ball bobbling past him into the net. How very fitting, and so impressively modern. The Sky Strikers World Cup isn't all about winning, it's about recognising different levels of achievement.

Prog Rock

It could only happen once in the history of the football programme, but what a time it was. Pure danger. Revolution, baby...

After a frustrating decade spent toeing the line, tapping out safe, sensibly stylish progs while the world around them blossomed and burned, the programme designers' union finally decided they'd had enough: no more covers with club badges or black-and-white aerial views of the ground. It was time to join the party. To let their collective hair down.

By the early '70s, pop art and psychedelia were last decade's thing. Prog rock, Bolshie political posterised images, glam grooves and furiously modern Penguin paperbacks were now where it was at in graphical design.

Time to get with-it. To experiment. To blur, bubble and blow up. You were either on the funky bus or off the funky bus, Mr Editor.

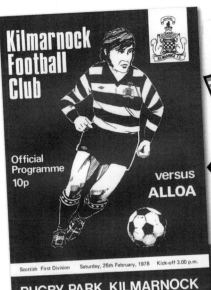

Kilmarnock Football Club

Official Programme 10p

versus ALLOA

Scottish First Division   Saturday, 25th February, 1978   Kick-off 3.00 p.m.

RUGBY PARK, KILMARNOCK

SOUTHAMPTON FOOTBALL CLUB

SOUTHAMPTON FC

OFFICIAL YEAR BOOK 1975|76

WEMBLEY SOUVENIR EDITION

60p

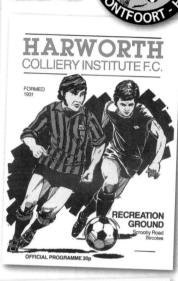

1946

V.V. MONTFOORT - HOLLAND

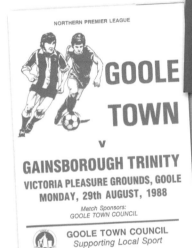

NORTHERN PREMIER LEAGUE

GOOLE TOWN

v

GAINSBOROUGH TRINITY

VICTORIA PLEASURE GROUNDS, GOOLE
MONDAY, 29th AUGUST, 1988

Match Sponsors:
GOOLE TOWN COUNCIL

GOOLE TOWN COUNCIL
Supporting Local Sport

Programme 30p

bobbing along

HARWORTH COLLIERY INSTITUTE F.C.

FORMED 1931

RECREATION GROUND
Scrooby Road
Bircotes

OFFICIAL PROGRAMME 20p

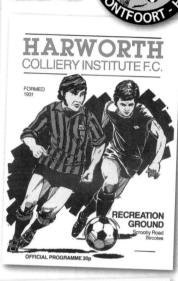

WEST HAM

SUPPORTER

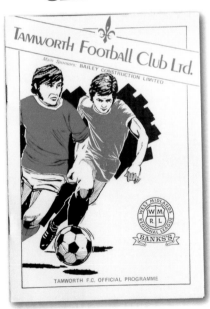

TAMWORTH Football Club Ltd.

Main Sponsors: BAILEY CONSTRUCTION LIMITED

WEST MIDLANDS REGIONAL LEAGUE

BANKS'S

TAMWORTH F.C. OFFICIAL PROGRAMME

DUMBARTON F.C.

OFFICIAL PROGRAMME – 20p

SCOTTISH LEAGUE DIVISION 1

Dumbarton v East Stirling
SATURDAY 29th AUGUST, 1981 — KICK-OFF 3.00 p.m.

The Sideburn Bob Feature

Throughout the final decades of the 20th century, a powerful phenomenon took root in football. Largely unnoticed, it spread as stealthily as the wafting smell of fried onions over terraces, burrowing into the subconscious of unsuspecting fans. The name of this creeping scourge? Clipart.

Originally in Letraset form, one popular set of generic images was then bundled with cheap computer packages. And that's how the only football graphic fit for purpose became a viral cult.

Oddly, the sheer ubiquity of the image was only recognised and made public recently, by non-League editor Tony Candland,

who christened his longtime companion 'Sideburn Bob'.

Bob and his mate 'Dependable Dave' have starred on programme covers, badges and handbooks, and they even crop up on the club crests of a couple of Continental clubs. But are they in on the joke?

The thing is, once you've noticed Bob, you can never unnotice him...

Football League Review

In its various forms, the *Football League Review* was a free weekly magazine ('5p where sold') that came stapled inside various club programmes in the '60s and '70s.

Not a lot of people know that it started life in 1965 as the *Soccer Review*, an independent magazine published in Leicester by Sport and Screen Productions. After one successful season appearing as an insert in a number of club programmes, it was taken over by the Football League, becoming much more widespread as the 'Official Journal' and tub-thumping mouthpiece of the League powerbrokers up in Lytham St Annes.

It's thanks to Hyder Jawad's debut *Soccerama* magazine that we found out this much about the *FLR*, always previously something

under review

of an enigma despite tatty piles of a few of its 366 issues appearing at every car boot sale.

"They printed and produced 100 million copies in just shy of a decade," Hyder reported, "creating a canon of work that involved 7,000 pages, two million words

and 300 colour team photographs."

Sadly the end came in 1974 when too few clubs were willing to absorb its increased printing costs.

The *FLR* still provides a brilliant snapshot of football life away from the glamour of the big clubs, being blessed with the work of

football's greatest documentary photographer, Peter Robinson.

The adverts for petrol, cars, beer and fags also conjure up a lost world. It's strangely touching to realise how earnestly we set about wrecking the planet and totalling our bodies. Hell, it was the '70s!

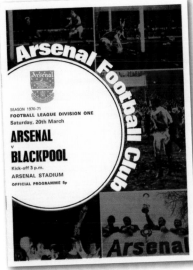

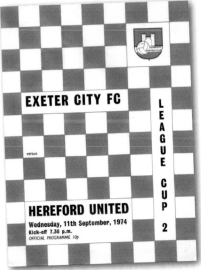

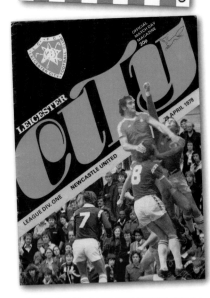

Copycats

As the editor of any football club programme in the '70s, exactly parallel limitations applied to your product as to the first-team manager's. With all due respect, there was little chance that Bristol City, Exeter City or Bury would sign Alan Ball for £220,000 and romp the League. Maverick talent and fresh ideas cost money most clubs could ill afford.

In the press office, just the same as out on the pitch, cloth had to be cut accordingly, along with a few corners that no one would ever notice. What chance mighty QPR ever visiting Exeter, after all?

Programme Tour of Britain

It's all aboard Paul Parker's big QPR hot-air balloon for a whistle-stop tour of Britain. So pull on your football kit, grab an Amish peasant girl... and chocks away!

We first float into the clouds over the Forth Road Bridge, an engineering feat so wondrous it graced the Hearts prog cover even before it opened for business in 1964. Drifting due west from Edinburgh, we next enjoy an aerial view of Greenock Municipal Buildings. Worth seeing, but not worth ballooning to see.

Floating south, England's first attractions are the Victorian floodlight pylon aka Blackpool Tower, and Clifford's Tower at York Castle. It's from the 13th century, when Cliff was young.

Interestingly, Grimsby Dock Tower isn't a lighthouse but a huge hydraulic water tower once used to power all the dock machinery. And the Radcliffe Camera, nestled amid Oxford's dreaming spires, isn't a camera but a library. It's time to land for a dependably classy sherbet at the Regency Queen's Hotel in Cheltenham.

On the picturesque south coast, the Gulls' cover view provides a subliminal message to Robin Stubbs, to smack it in the lobster pot – more use than cliffs and pier views. Then it's back to the Smoke in time for *EastEnders*, floating into the Isle of Dogs and Millwall territory over Tower Bridge. It may be a bumpy landing...

KEY TO
TH-INCH MAP
SECTIONS

uter Hebrides, Orkney and
tland on Tenth-Inch Scale)

Scale 1:3,000,000

No. 2099

Greenock Morton

Scottish League—1st Division
Monday, 3rd January, 1966

ST. MIRREN

OFFICIAL PROGRAMME · 6d

*The Management and Players wish you all
A Happy New Year*

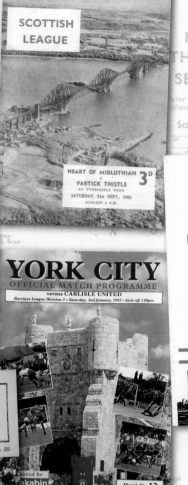

HEART OF MIDLOTHIAN
OFFICIAL PROGRAMME

SCOTTISH
LEAGUE

HEART OF MIDLOTHIAN
v
PARTICK THISTLE
AT TYNECASTLE PARK
SATURDAY, 21st SEPT., 1963
KICK-OFF 3 P.M.

3d

SEASIDERS SCENE
OFFICIAL MATCH PROGRAMME

TODAY'S MATCH SPONSOR:
Guardian Royal Exchange Sports and Social Club
SATURDAY, 11th MAY, 1985
WREXHAM
Kick-off 3.00 p.m.
PROGRAMME PRICE 40p

THE MARINER
GRIMSBY TOWN FOOTBALL CLUB LTD.

FOOTBALL LEAGUE
THIRD DIVISION

SATURDAY, NOVEMBER 19th 1966
SWANSEA TOWN
KICK-OFF 3 P.M.

PRICE SIXPENCE

YORK CITY
OFFICIAL MATCH PROGRAMME
versus CARLISLE UNITED
Barclays League Division 3 - Saturday, 2nd January, 1993 - kick-off 3.00pm

Match No 12
£1.00

A-plan
For Motor, Life, and All Insurance
A-PLAN INSURANCE, 117 HIGH ST., OXFORD
TEL. 41441 - PRIVATE EXCHANGE — DAY AND NIGHT SERVICE
HEAD OFFICE: LLOYDS AVENUE, CITY OF LONDON
BRANCHES THROUGHOUT THE COUNTRY

Official Programme—Price One Shilling   Volume 21, No. 25

FOOTBALL LEAGUE
2nd DIVISION

UNITED v LEICESTER CITY
GOOD FRIDAY, 27 MARCH, 1970. Kick-off 3 p.m.

SHERGOLDS
THE DEPARTMENTAL IRONMONGERS OF HEADINGTON
—have so much to offer!—after the match wander through our stores (87 London
Road) and see for yourself. WALLPAPERS · PAINTS · TOOLS · DOMESTIC-
WARE · GARDEN TOOLS & FURNITURE etc.
ALSO AT:
COWLEY CENTRE · WITNEY · SUMMERTOWN · ABINGDON · CIRENCESTER

Take a trip with Paul
Parker, floating south
from the Firth of Forth
to Old Father Thames.

GM THE GM VAUXHALL CONFERENCE   Gulf CLUB MAIN SPONSOR

CHELTENHAM TOWN FOOTBALL CLUB

DARLINGTON

70p

MILLWALL

v
Queens Park Rangers
FOOTBALL LEAGUE
SATURDAY, 8th FEBRUARY, 1964
KICK OFF 3-15 p.m.
Official Programme Sixpence

Torquay United A.F.C.
OFFICIAL PROGRAMME

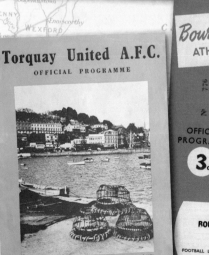

TORQUAY UNITED
v.
STOCKPORT COUNTY
SATURDAY, 20th OCTOBER, 1962
Kick-off 3.00 p.m.

Threepence
No 1553

Bournemouth & Boscombe
ATHLETIC FOOTBALL CLUB

No 776

OFFICIAL
PROGRAMME

3d

TUESDAY, DECEMBER 27th, 1960
BOURNEMOUTH AND BOSCOMBE
versus
READING
FOOTBALL LEAGUE, DIVISION III
KICK-OFF 2.15 p.m.

ALBION
news

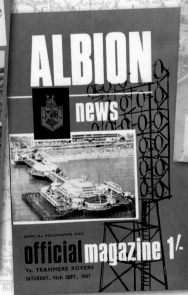

OFFICIAL PROGRAMME AND
official magazine 1/-

vs. TRANMERE ROVERS
SATURDAY, 16th SEPT., 1967

Burnley

Champs in Miniature

At first glance, you might assume Corgi Toys were taking liberties with their

contemporary 1962 tribute to Burnley's victory parade through town after winning the League. So we took it on ourselves to check up, and in fact it's surprisingly accurate.

The actual Burlingham Seagull coach was hung with those exact banners. Strangest of all, Jimmy Adamson, and team-mates really did pop up through a large hole in the single deckers' roof. Now we're researching hard to find out what they were standing on, or whether they were hovering in mid-air.

Celtic

Ouch!

After the glory of Lisbon in 1967, it's easy to forget Celtic's second tilt at the European Cup, which

caricaturist Malky McCormick's vicious '70s style.

Bertie Auld looks like one

ended in defeat to Feyenoord in the 1970 final in Milan.

Even so, the *Sunday Mail*'s commemorative poster was a bit harsh in getting its revenge in first, featuring legendary

of the Ant Hill Mob from *Wacky Races*. Bobby Murdoch is an evil balloon. Jimmy Johnstone is fully one foot tall. And poor old 'Yogi' Hughes.

It could never happen now.

Cardiff City

Friends in High Places

As an enthusiastic card collector of junior-school age it never occurred to me to question the selection of teams that appeared in A&BC's iconic purple-back series of 1971/72.

But now my attention has finally been drawn to the jokers in the pack of cards – for so

many years hidden in full view – I'm duty bound to blow the whistle.

Let's go back and check which teams made the cut.

There's 20 First Division sides from last season, minus relegated Burnley and Blackpool, plus Leicester and Sheffield United, fresh up from Division Two.

And then there's Cardiff City, frankly undeserving having only come third in the Second Division.

Never mind who gifted the World Cup to Qatar. It's time questions were asked in Parliament about Cardiff City's friends in high places.

Charlton Athletic

Valley Girls

Here's a tantalising glimpse of the rosettes, sports bags, scarves and pennants in the window of the Valley Shop. As the Athletic girls test their sales techniques, three avid Valiants fans are unintentionally caught by the snapper: one young herbert and an elderly herbert are both transfixed, one by awakening, the other by memories. A third herbert has bought himself a rattle, and remains otherwise unimpressed.

Coventry City

College Cazh

Further to our trainspotters' guide to football neckwear on page 32, here's one we forgot. In between the trad bar scarf and the printed silk jobbie came a nationwide trend for the stripy college-style scarf.

This wonderful example has collected up a splendid extra layer of cloth sew-on patches, from Sky Blue boots and 'Ace of Clubs' boasts to Victory Vs and thumbs-up, all dating from a period of unbridled and fully justified optimism at Highfield Road.

If anyone would like to swap for the owners' two doubles or help him fill his long-standing bald spot, get in touch and we'll be happy to act as football agents at the going rate.

Chelsea

Blue Books

Albert Sewell blazed a trail as Chelsea's programme editor from 1948 to '78, introducing colour pictures and setting a trend as he transformed a glorified teamsheet into one of the first feature-packed matchday magazines.

Similarly groundbreaking, his books for the hot Chelsea brand sadly charted a temporary downward spiral from FA Cup and Euro glory via the drying-up of trophies to relegation in 1974/75. RIP Albert Sewell MBE, 1927-2018.

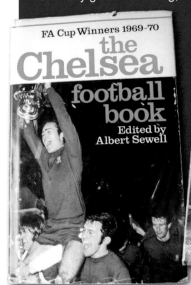

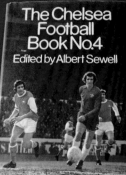

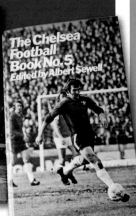

Crystal Palace

True Colours

For a series of kits that offered so little in terms of consistency, Palace's curious progression throughout the '60s and '70s has achieved cult status among neutral admirers.

We're not even sure that claret, blue and yellow constitute a legit choice as club colours; they just happen to look great.

Never a club to rest on their laurels, the lairy pinstripes were ditched in 1972 for twin central stripes on an Ajax-ish pattern, before the claret and blue were inched apart in unique style.

Imagine Palace fans' surprise in '73 when new boss Big Mal plumped for a red-and-blue stripe look inspired by Bayern Munich.

All this, and the cool sash of '76 still to look forward to!

CRYSTAL PALACE
Jim Scott
INSIDE LEFT

CRYSTAL PALACE
IAIN PHILLIP

CRYSTAL PALACE
PETER TAYLOR
MIDFIELD

Derby County

Under the Counter

Serious Subbuteo collectors: continue reading about this item at your own risk. Here's a vintage 'heavyweight' team

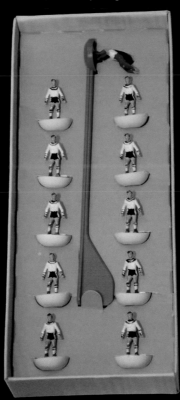

likely to result in paroxysms of jealousy and frustration as you attempt to work out its origin.

Back in the Rams' heyday, when Cloughie's side wore black multi-banded collars, cuffs and sock-tops between 1969 and '71, this classic team was made in very limited numbers for sale exclusively in sports and toyshops in Derbyshire.

The variation doesn't appear in any official Subbuteo catalogue, but did come complete in a Subbuteo box of the era, clearly marked 'Derby County'.

Everton

Choons

In the mid '80s Everton found themselves with a near-perfect hit-rate of success. And they weren't bad on the pitch, either.

The synthtastic Cup final

EVERTON
Cup Squad
THE BOYS IN BLUE

EVERTON 1985
THE OFFICIAL TEAM RECORD

HERE WE GO

single for '84 may have sounded a bit flat, but it carried Howard Kendall's boys through against Watford at Wembley, setting a dangerous precedent. Despite marking a lyrical nadir, 'Here We Go' was responsible for the Toffees romping the League and the ECWC. Shockingly, the next Cup final 45 resulted in a loss to Liverpool – but the record was a slow burner, and order was restored with the League win in 1986/87.

EVERTON
FOOTBALL TEAM 1986
Everybody's Cheering the Blues

comic cuts

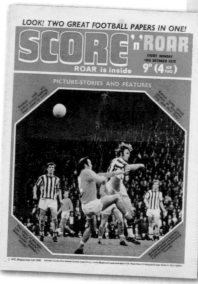

Great News for All Readers!

Just how satisfying would it be to see a massive family-tree graphic that featured every comic that existed in the late 20th century, charting the way old favourites have a habit of eating up new pretenders every few years.

At the top, you'd have the classics of the early and mid '60s. In this unthinkable period of prehistory, even *Tiger* and *Jag* (not forgetting *Hurricane*) were separate entities, along with countless other comics remembered for their subsequent enforced marriages. *Lion*. *Champion*. *Eagle*. *Thunder*. Before they became *Lion & Champion*, *Lion & Thunder*, *Lion & Eagle*. And eventually no *Lion* at all.

Who doesn't remember that fateful Saturday morning when you saw the dreaded cover splash – 'Great news for all readers!' – that meant your favourite comic was going to 'join forces' with one that you didn't like half as much!

Then, the next week, the awful sensation of becoming a subtitle. Imagine the shame of *Valiant*,

having eaten *Knockout*, *Vulcan* and *TV21* and hit the heights hosting gypsy winger 'Raven on the Wing', when the next cannibalistic incorporation saw the sad flip to *Battle & Valiant*.

So, back to the subject of that sprawling, all-encompassing family tree. No, we haven't doodled away the past seven years mapping it all out; but here's a chunk out of the middle that features the classic football comics.

By the dawn of the '70s, *Jag* had been shrunken in stature to

54

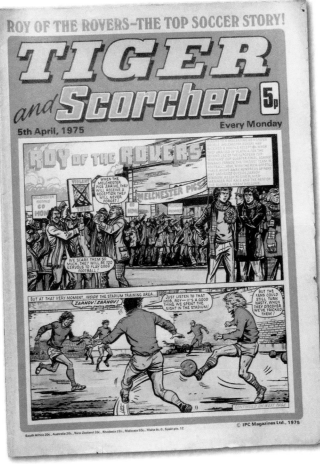

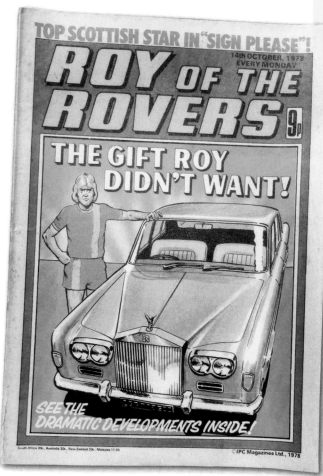

around half a square inch on the cover of *Tiger*, 'Football Family Robinson' its only survivor among *Tiger* staples such as 'Roy of the Rovers' and a retrospectively odd mix of sporting heroes. 'Philip Driver, Golf Spy'. Redskin wrestler, Johnny Cougar. And 'Martin's Marvellous Mini'.

The popular new *Scorcher* was doing brisk business on the back of football's first marketing boom, with 'Bobby of the Blues' as flagship story alongside school-team goalie 'Peter the Cat' and

brilliant northern urchin, 'Nipper'.

Without doubt the strangest market entry at this time was *Score 'n' Roar* – a curious Siamese twin of a comic, born incorporating two titles, *Roar* tucked away in the centre staples of its sibling. Solid centre-half 'Jack of United' was lead strip while groovy brother 'Jimmy of City' banged glam goals deeper inside.

If there were relatively few tears shed with the consolidation of *Scorcher & Score*, the adult world still judged the market cluttered.

The shock creation of *Tiger & Scorcher* in 1974 signalled the untimely disappearance of dear friends such as Ted Legge of 'Lags Eleven' and 'The Kangaroo Kid'.

Unthinkable, even now.

The only truly great bit of news for all readers came in 1976 with the announcement of *Roy of the Rovers* comic, which for once didn't involve any asset stripping. Instead, it ran concurrently with *Tiger & Scorcher*, spawning a new generation of heroes for kids a couple of years younger.

Character Study

Isn't it strange how the comic characters that inhabited the imaginary world of every youthful football fan tend to linger in the memory so much more vividly than potentially useful information such as our children's birthdays, MOT dates and so on?

Any psychoanalyst would struggle to explain the disproportionate number of times that Billy Dane arises in conversation between men of a certain age. Billy was just a schoolkid. He wasn't a sexy world-beater and role model like Roy of the Rovers, but instead an everyboy like ourselves – until he pulled on the football boots he'd found in his nan's attic, once the property of vintage goalscorer 'Dead Shot' Keen. Maybe the story's message was about inner confidence, and that we all have the innate ability to succeed if we believe in ourselves. Or maybe it was about haunted boots. Either way, Billy's eponymous footwear

has a spooky tendency to arise even today whenever a player changes his boots on the pitch, or a five-a-side team-mate turns up with knackered old trainers.

In the same way, every 'hard man' defender is compared by a certain demographic to Danefield United's brutish Johnny Dexter. Scottish goalkeepers are forever destined to look slightly confused at repeated mentions of Gordon Stewart of Tynefield City, aka 'The Safest Hands in Soccer' – a

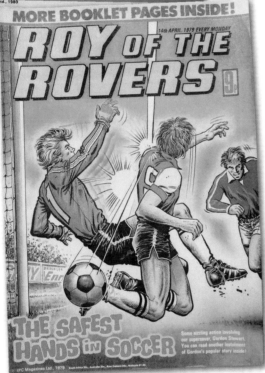

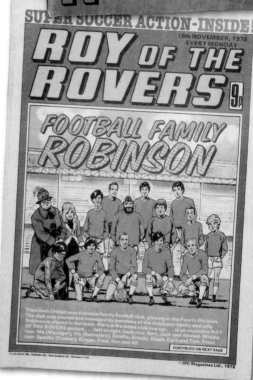

It was tough to explain how Gordon Stewart had spawned his son, Rick, apparently around the age of nine.

mantle later assumed (after a fatal air crash and a wobble in the timeline) by Gordon's son, Rick, of Tynefield United. And, naturally, eyebrows are raised in expectation every time your team signs a 7-foot Herculean forward from a Scottish Second Division side.

Some of us still wait, as trusting and as hopeful as ever, for a struggling basement-league club to be bought out by a family (so far, so credible) who then proceed to populate the team solely from

within their own number, each exhibiting physical characteristics that can be summed up (by bullies and body shamers) in one word. Specky. Grizzly. Tich. Giraffe. Bowler Hat Bloke. (That's three). More likely to turn up in reality is the story of the school side gifted a pitch and clubhouse by a farmer. Hmm, 'Tommy's Troubles' were pretty much over whenever he sold the land for development, in true lower-league style.

The graphic drama of 'Mike's

Mini Men' was most infused with social realism. School boarder Mike Dailey's attempts to set up a Subbuteo league (though the S word was never uttered in the strip) ended up in a fist fight with older boys who wanted to use the games room for table tennis. It proper went off. And then there were lessons for us all to learn when Mike was chosen to represent Great Britain in a tournament in London, and the oppo locked him in a cupboard.

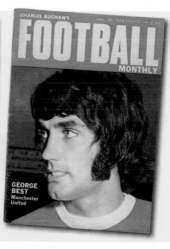

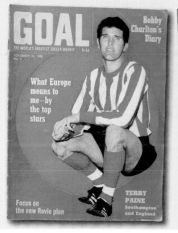

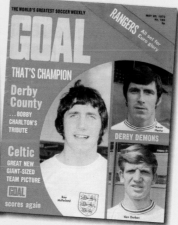

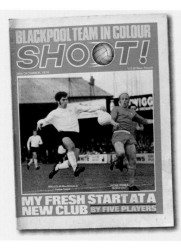
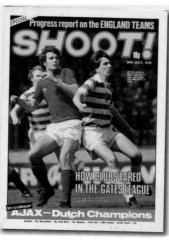

Our Back Pages

Having emerged in 1951 as the UK's first recognisable football magazine, you may locate *Charles Buchan's Football Monthly* deep in the forbidding magazine shelves of history, or otherwise as a close nostalgic friend, colourful and groundbreaking. For those who remember its heyday it's usually an eternal favourite, initially offering insights into the game and players' lives behind the scenes alongside adverts for Brylcreem and sturdy boots in the pre-war style.

Credited with creating the template for every football mag that followed, *CB*'s duly suffered once a slew of younger, hipper World Cup-crazed rivals popped up. 'The World's Greatest Football Weekly', they used to call it – yes, even after the launch of Jimmy Hill's eponymous glossy periodical in sunny 1967. But then came *Goal* in 1968. Pow! Feel the impact of that cool pop-art cover, the promise of star chat and a burgeoning choice of small-ad gimmicks – quickly followed in

1969 by another IPC title, *Shoot!* The 'terrific new football paper for boys' boasted star writers, 'You Are The Ref', 'Focus On', 'Football Funnies'... All this and free football league ladders, too.

Even though *Goal*'s circulation kept growing to a pinnacle of 200,000 in 1971, when it came to the inevitable crunch, there was no surprise when the resultant title was *Shoot! incorporating Goal*, the victorious title continuing to thrive into the new millennium.

The chief reason for its eventual

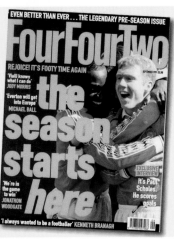

demise was the September 1979 launch of Emap's *Match* magazine, whose spangly look, dramatic covers and big, borderless pages offered a fresh, youthful appeal. The staid questions from *Shoot!*'s Q&A were supplanted by more chatty queries about team-mates and players' lifestyles, with music and games and gossip pushing in and proving that football fans don't just like football. It may have felt a bit garish to older teens, but *Match* had staying power, overtaking and then doubling

Shoot!'s sales during the '90s. It just recently celebrated its 40th birthday, becoming the longest-running UK football mag.

IPC's *90 Minutes* started off as a surprisingly serious read, but under the stewardship of editor Paul Hawksbee soon found a uniquely '90s niche, pitched between the irreverent, arsey, fan-friendly fanzine market and the burgeoning lad mag scene led by *Loaded*. Back issues still stand up today, which is rare praise for any 20-year-old magazine.

Haymarket's *FourFourTwo* was always a more staid, steady option, perhaps reflecting the company's founding by Michael Heseltine. In truth we're a bit biased, but there were countless memorable features and maverick moments in Teddington over 24 years before the mag was sold to Future in 2018. Then, to cap it all, they only went and let former *Loaded* editor, James Brown, take over the reins for five issues. Allegedly, anarchy ensued. But hey, what did they expect? Charles Buchan?

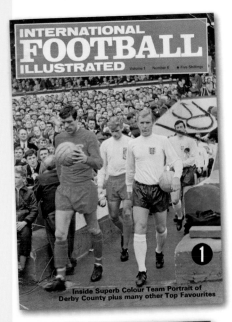

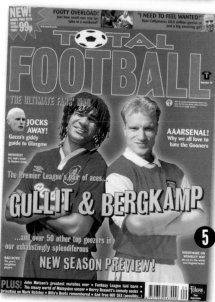

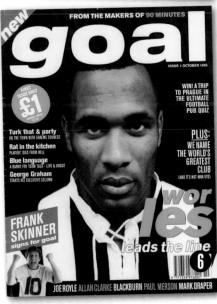

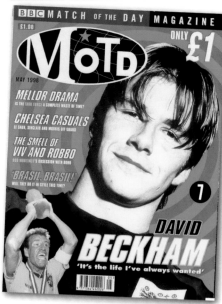

Spoilt for Choice

The final stretches of the 20th century will go down in history as a magazine boom time, with football fans served by a wide range of passionate and eccentric, if short-lived, titles.

1 – *International Football Ilustrated* belonged to a time when huge Technicolor action shots were still rare in monochrome football reporting. It's like you could walk right inside some of these images.

2 – *Striker* dived into the market led by *Shoot!* and *Goal* in 1970. Sparse attractions included 'The Soccer World of Colin Bell' and club-by-club features; but by 1972 it was last in, first out.

3 – Sister paper to the Donny Osmond- and Marc Bolan-friendly *Music Star*. Never too keen on words, it was fun to see our less likely candidates for sex-god status given the glam rock treatment. Maybe if they'd just concentrated on the players who grew big sideys?

4 – Published by PR Publications in Alvechurch, the *FT* was earnest but seemed out of time by the '80s. 'News Through the Divisions' rarely got you too fired up. A curate's egg from when there wasn't much competition around.

5 – The *Loaded*-led lad-mag rush resulted in a '90s glut. Future's *Total Football* had depth, quirkiness and moments aplenty. Not so sure about Photoshopping heads on to cover stars' bodies...

6 – IPC's revival of the *Goal* title, led by *90 Minutes* supremo Paul Hawksbee, was another success in a crowded market, with attitude, ideas and proper writing. But look out, everyone, here comes the net.

7 – Sign o' the Times Alert! There's a girl fan stripping off, flick-book style, in the corner of each page of this subsidised spin-off BBC production.

Our Favourite Shop

English Football was at a very low ebb when John Gaustad decided to test his theory that there would be room in the market for a bookshop devoted to sports titles.

It was a brave decision for the New Zealander, who mortgaged his house to open Sportspages on Caxton Walk, just off the Charing Cross Road. In September 1985 football was still reeling from Millwall's riot at Luton, the Bradford fire and Heysel. But John's hunch proved to be right, and people were soon flocking to the place where they knew that hard-to-find book on football, baseball or yoga would be in stock.

Within a year *When Saturday Comes* launched and was swiftly followed by dozens and then hundreds of fanzines. Somehow, room was found to stock them all and Sportpages became a fanzine mecca. In the age before Twitter, or even the radio phone-in, we had no idea what fans of other clubs were thinking. It was a wonderful eye-opener, not only catching the *zeitgeist* perfectly but also helping to shape it.

No trip to London was complete without a visit to the shop that felt like home, picking out a tenners' worth of fanzines and poring over them in the café opposite.

Sadly, the rise of rents and the internet saw Sportspages go out of business in 2005, but John's landmark venture will always be remembered as a game changer.

TOWN GAY MEADOW

Chairman: H.S. Yates
Coach: Post vacant
Secretary: M.J. Starkey
Captain: Jake King
Colours: Amber & blue

TREVOR JONES

JAKE KING

COLIN GRIFFIN

CARL LEONARD

...er club. ■0, □0. Defender. Ht.5.10.Wt.11.0. No other club. ■39, □6.

Defender. Ht.6.0. Wt. 11.7. Derby County. ■46, □2.

Defender. Ht.5.9.Wt.10.3. No other club. ■26, □0.

...MY GAY

DAVID TONG

TREVOR BIRCH

STEVE BIGGINS

...Wt. 12.0. ...30, □0. Midfield. Ht. 5.8. Wt. 10.1. Blackpool. ■37, □5.

Forward. Ht.5.11.Wt.11.13. Liverpool. ■14, □2.

Forward. Ht.6.0.Wt.11.12. No other club. ■45, □9.

ROKER PARK

Chairman: K.I. Collings
Coach: Frank Clark
Secretary: R.M. Linney
Captain: Mike Docherty
Colours: Red & white

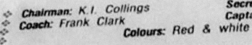

JEFF CLARKE

JOE BOLTON

MICK DOCHERTY

...efender. Ht.5.11.Wt.12.1. ...nchester City. ■34, □2.

Defender. Ht.5.11. Wt. 11.12. No other club. ■32, □3.

Defender. Ht.5.6.Wt.9.8. Manchester City. ■27, □4.

SWANSEA CITY

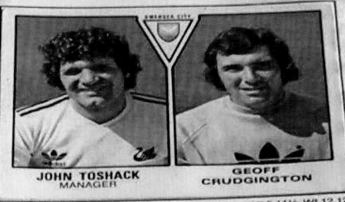

JOHN TOSHACK
MANAGER

GEOFF CRUDGINGTON

BRIAN ATTLEY

Player-manager since Feb. '78, formerly player at Liverpool.

Goalkeeper. Ht.5.11½.Wt.12.12. Crewe Alexandra. ■46,□0.

Defender. Ht.5.9.Wt.9. Cardiff City. ■20,□1.

JOHN MAHONEY

TOMMY CRAIG

JEREM CHARLI

Midfield. Ht.5.7½.Wt.11.4. 'Boro. ■0,□0.●44,●1 (W)

Midfield. Ht.5.7½.Wt.11.7. Aston Villa. ■0,□0.●1,●0(S).

Midfield. Ht.6.1.Wt. other club. ■40,□

WATFORD

GRAHAM TAYLOR
MANAGER

STEVE SHERWOOD

Manager since June '77, formerly manager with Lincoln C.

Goalkeeper. Ht. 6.3. Wt. 15.0. Chelsea. ■16,□0.

Defender. No other cl

MARTIN CHIVERS
Inside left
SOUTHAMPTON

GORDON BANKS
Goalkeeper
STOKE CITY

GEORGE BEST

30 RON YEATS

Centre half

LIVERPOOL

Previously with Dundee United, he joined Liverpool in 1962. Capped twice for Scotland, he is captain of Liverpool and scored 2 goals last season in 41 League games.

COLLECT THE SET
of 5½" x 3½"
FULL COLOUR PIN-UPS OF ENGLANDS' STARS

67/68 Black Backs

Q.P.R.
INSIDE LEFT
RODNEY MARSH

FULHAM
INSIDE LEFT
FRANK LARGE

LIVERPOOL
OUTSIDE RIGHT
IAN CALLAGHAN

COLIN BELL
I. RIGHT   MANCHESTER C.
5ft 11½ins. 11st 4lbs   Born Hesleden

A brilliant young inside-forward, Bell was signed from Bury in March 1966 for £45,000, which was then a record fee for a teenager. His consistent creative play since then has been a feature of City's football, and he has been capped for England's Under 23 team.

FOOTBALL QUIZ
What is the record F.A. Cup Final score?

FOR MAGIC ANSWER - Rub edge of coin over blank space.

Printed in England   **77**

68/69 Yellow Backs

FRANK CASPER   CENTRE
Burnley   FORWARD

VIC MOBLEY   CENTRE
SHEFFIELD WEDNESDAY   HALF

PETER KNOWLES   INSIDE
WOLVERHAMPTON   LEFT
WANDERERS

JOHN O'ROURKE   LEFT
34   IPSWICH TOWN   INSIDE
HT: 5ft. 9ins. WT: 11st. Born Northampton.

Joined Ipswich in February, 1968, and scored 12 goals in the final fifteen matches leading to promotion. Formerly with Arsenal, Chelsea, Luton Town and Middlesborough, he has already been capped for England's Under-23 side.

FOOTBALL QUIZ
WHO WON THE FIRST WORLD CUP TOURNAMENT?

URUGUAY, In 1930.
Printed in England   ANSWER

69/70 Green Backs

BLACKPOOL

Glyn James
CENTRE HALF

ARSENAL

Charlie George
INSIDE FORWARD

NEWCASTLE UNITED

Frank Clark
FULL BACK

IAM McFAUL   16
NEWCASTLE UNITED
HEIGHT: 5' 8½" WEIGHT: 12st. 9lb. BORN COLERAINE

One of the most improved goalkeepers in the First Division, McFaul's brilliant form is one of the reasons for the tightness of the Newcastle defence. Signed from Linfield in November, 1966, he took over the United's first team two years later when Gordon Marshall was transferred to Nottingham Forest.

KNOW YOUR TEAM
Everton
Formed: 1878
Ground: Goodison Park.
Capacity: 63,900
Nickname:
Ground Record: 78,299
v Liverpool, Sept. 1948.

FOOTBALLER

70/71 Orange Backs

The Greatest A&BC Poll

Crikey, was it really six years ago that we conducted the football card poll to end all football card polls? A poll so conclusive it could easily have been officiated over by top football referee, Graham Poll?

Our aim was clear and pure: to find out which was the greatest ever set of A&BC football cards. Our method was state of art at the time and impossible to fix: the fleetingly overused poll buttons on our Got, Not Got blog site.

Ignoring all of the earlier A&BC series because we're too young to remember them, even as hand-me-downs, and skirting past the commonly held conclusion that every bloke's favourite football card set is simply his first, we can now proudly publish our findings, as topical as ever.

In reverse order, 15% of the vote

WEST BROMWICH ALBION

TONY BROWN
WING HALF

TOTTENHAM HOTSPUR

ROGER MORGAN
WINGER

LEICESTER CITY

GRAHAM CROSS
WING HALF

TED HEMSLEY
SHEFFIELD UNITED

HEIGHT: 5' 9½" WEIGHT: 11st. 4lb. BORN: STOKE

A valuable member of the Sheffield United defence, Hemsley played 234 games for Shrewsbury before his transfer, and is now firmly established at Bramhall Lane. A swift tackler, his distribution from defence is good, and he supports the attack well.

DID YOU KNOW?
Ted plays cricket in the summer for Worcester

CARD No. 180

71/72 Purple Backs

NORWICH CITY

GRAHAM PADDON
MID-FIELD

WEST HAM

CLYDE BEST
STRIKER

HUDDERSFIELD

DICK KRYZWICKI
MID-FIELD

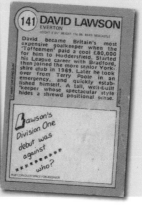

(141) DAVID LAWSON
EVERTON

HEIGHT: 6' 2½" WEIGHT: 11st. 8lb. BORN: NEWCASTLE

David became Britain's most expensive goalkeeper when the 'Toffeemen' paid a cool £80,000 for him to Huddersfield. Started his League career with Bradford, then joined the more senior Yorkshire club in 1969. Later he took over from Terry Poole in an emergency, and quickly established himself. A tall, well-built 'keeper whose spectacular style hides a shrewd positional sense.

Lawson's Division One debut was against ********* who?

72/73 Orange-red Backs

EVERTON

ROD BELFITT

CRYSTAL PALACE

ALAN WHITTLE

MAN. CITY

TONY BOOK

104 CHRIS LAWLER

TEAM: Liverpool | POSITION: Backfour
HEIGHT: 6' 0" WEIGHT: 12st 10lb BORN: Liverpool
LAST CLUB: None | GOALS: None
HONOURS: Full England, Under-23, Youth & Schoolboy Caps. League, F.A. Cup Winners medals.

Hard to pinpoint the merits of this brilliant player with a weak spot. So conscious he has scored over 60 goals, it has missed only one match for Liverpool.

73/74 Blue Backs

MIDDLESBRO'

ALAN FOGGON

CHELSEA

RON HARRIS

LEEDS UTD.

BILLY BREMNER

PETER SHILTON (68)
LEICESTER CITY

Succeeded Gordon Banks as No. 1 choice for Leicester and later took over from the same player as England's goalkeeper. Has won schools, youth, Under-23 honours as well. Made his debut in 1966 before he turned professional.
Ht. 6.0 Born Leicester
Wt. 12.10 Pos. Goalkeeper
Last Club Leicester C.

AGAINST WHOM DID HE MAKE HIS LEAGUE DEBUT AT 16?

RUB COIN OVER SPACE FOR ANSWER

74/75 Red-orange Backs

gave third place to the blue backs of '73, with their lairy Art Deco team-name banners.

In second place with 16.5% was the green-back set of 1969, which came complete with a black-and-white 'crinkle-cut' player photograph in every pack.

And the official greatest ever A&BC – with their sumptuous oversize feel, their ace mix of player portraits and training ground shots, their magical 'rub with side of coin' quiz teaser, and freebie Superstar Posters – were… the 1970/71 orange backs!

Got, Not Got: Ronnie the Junior Blade checks out his FKS Mexico 70 requirements.

The Wonderful World of FKS

If ever there were a sticker series aptly named, it was FKS's long-running Wonderful World of Soccer Stars. Never before or certainly since has such a curious assortment of images found its way on to a set of cards or stickers. Here we would find the stars of the '60s and '70s not only 'in action' (as promised in the extended title of the 1969/70 edition), but also larking around in pre-season photo-shoots, running out of the tunnel, training half-heartedly or plain old posing for head-and-shoulders shots.

It was precisely this make-do-and-mend, cutting-room floor quality that lent the stickers their timeless appeal, affording a glimpse into the excitement of Saturday afternoons alongside sneak peeks behind the scenes. The collected FKS library of images also gave us a flavour of the fast-changing world of football – whether it was in the creative techniques used by the picture editors as they struggled to keep up with transfers, or ultimately in the sense that the soccer industry was outgrowing the small, independent merch manufacturer such as FKS and their cardboard equivalent, A&BC.

By the end of the '70s, the writing was on the wall for unofficial club souvenirs, for unregulated local photographers and lovably amateurish sticker albums. Before too long complete

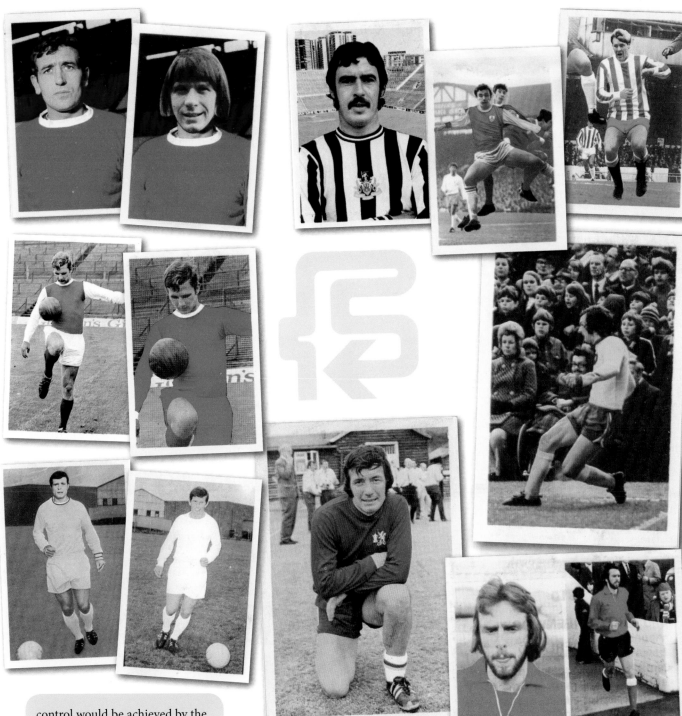

control would be achieved by the industry within the uniform pages of the Panini album.

Never again would we see the head of Man United's Shay Brennan transplanted with that of John Fitzpatrick. Long before digital editing, Jack Whitham's inconvenient switch from Sheff Wed to Liverpool was once easy to remedy with a touch-up brush, a technique that worked fine so long as the artist didn't recolour blue the shorts of Stoke's Tony Allen (sadly overlooking those of his team-mate) – or attempt to turn Leeds United's Johnny Giles into Cov's Dietmar Bruck. As for the Burnley sticker featuring Colin

Blant, we'll probably never find out how four teams came to be playing that day.

One unique FKS bonus was the ability to peer right inside the Wonderful World. Name a modern sticker outfit that might give you the chance to spot Basil Fawlty towering above the crowd at a Norwich City match, to discover that Newcastle play at the San Siro, or follow a wedding fight going on behind Chelsea's John Boyle. Best of all, you could even gatecrash the stickers

yourself, lurking as Sunderland's Roy Greenwood trotted out of the tunnel. And then repeating the trick with Billy Hughes.

costa packet

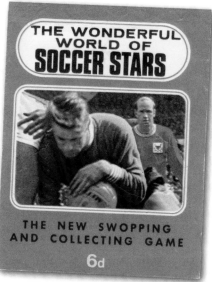

FFS: The company that taught us to spell swapping with an 'o'. My English teacher didn't agree.

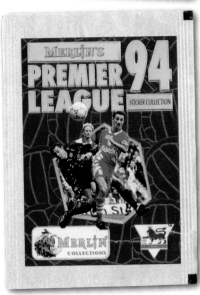

Throwing It All Away

Sorry to be a killjoy, but here's the indisputable proof that it just isn't possible. Apologies for taking the shine off a perfectly enjoyable day, so far. But the next time you get into that thoughtful pub/office conversation about the possibility of time travel, it ends here with this hard fact.

If it were possible for anyone, ever, to travel back in time, they'd already be among us – and the world would be full of beaming playboy millionaires instead of blokes who used to collect football cards when they were kids.

If only we'd known. If only we could have used our imaginations *and somehow guessed.*

It wasn't the teetering pile of football cards, kept in pristine condition for posterity, that was ever going to be worth enough money to change your life. It wasn't your complete rows of Panini stickers, or even the early World Cup issues you kept mint in a folder with your virgin album.

All the time, you held your fortune right in your hand. Then you ripped it up and threw it away.

That's right. It wasn't the cards or stickers that you needed to cling on to, it was all of your mates' hundreds of disposable wrappers crammed into the playground bin. Thirty quid per sixpenny packet.

Gah, what chance did we have of stopping our lucky windfall from slipping through our fingers when we never even noticed how Panini used the same packet design for whole decades on the trot?

Want to reach in and rip open a brand new packet of FKS gold stickers? Sometimes life just isn't fair.

counter culture

Manna from Heaven

Now let's leave behind the orbit of the regular card/sticker collector and move on to a previously unimagined world of rarity, value and privilege.

Where you or I would be chuffed to come across a common error card, a variation or empty sticker packet, there's a whole other class of collector with the uncanny ability to cross over to the other side of the counter, sourcing promotional material, display boxes and untouched treasure troves of unopened packets. How and where do they find it all? Only they will ever know.

If quality vintage football memorabilia has proven to be one of the best long-term investments of all, right up there with printer ink and Bitcoins, then every impossibly rare item of this internal card-industry material is a 24-carat pure gold nugget.

Feast your eyes on these ancient counter boxes, probably hidden away for years in warehouses full of old and dead stock, slowly multiplying in value.

What about the posters that were supposed to be destined for a corner-shop window 30 or 40 years ago? By what insane chain of events did they ever survive?

And so to the disposable inducements sent out by card manufacturers direct to your newsagent, promising the chance to win a Hillman Avenger for flogging us the cards we loved.

EVERTON

NIL SATIS NISI OPTIMUM

KEITH BERTSCHIN

WILLIE YOUNG
ARSENAL

MARK LAWRENSON
BRIGHTON & HOVE A.

I SWOP FIGURINE PANINI

Scottish League
QUEEN'S PARK
First Division

BOB LATCHFORD
SWANSEA CITY

KENNY HIBBITT
WOLVERHAMPTON W.

SUNDERLAND
COLIN WEST

FOOTBALL 78
FOOTBALL 79
FOOTBALL 80
PANINI'S FOOTBALL
PANINI'S FOOTBALL 82
PANINI'S FOOTBALL 83
FOOTBALL 84
PANINI'S FOOTBALL 85
PANINI'S FOOTBALL 86
FOOTBALL 87
PANINI'S FOOTBALL 88 STICKER ALBUM
PANINI FOOTBALL 89 STICKER ALBUM
FOOTBALL 1991
FOOTBALL 90 THE OFFICIAL STICKER COLLECTION
english FOOTBALL 92
FOOTBALL 93 STICKER ALBUM

Queen's Park provided all 11 players for Scotland's first international. But not many since.

Going for Gold

In these days when 11 year olds aren't so easily impressed, it's difficult to convey the enormity of the shockwave created by Panini's 'Football 78' collection.

An inspired bit of marketing saw the album intially given away with *Shoot!* magazine. Once you'd opened it up and put in that first free packet of stickers you were powerless to resist the urge to complete the set.

For kids brought up on FKS's *Wonderful World of Soccer* albums, this represented a quantum leap. The stickers were actually stickers, no more messy sessions with glue. Two pages for every club, including a teamgroup, manager and, best of all, the gold foil badge

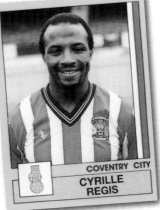

GARY BRIGGS — OXFORD UNITED — WANG

CYRILLE REGIS — COVENTRY CITY

stick with it

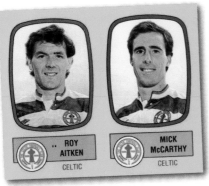

ROY AITKEN — CELTIC

MICK McCARTHY — CELTIC

NOTTINGHAM FOREST

MILLWALL — TERRY HURLOCK

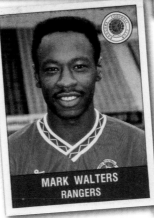

MARK WALTERS — RANGERS

FOOTBALL — WIMBLEDON — HANS SEGERS

TONY DALEY — ASTON VILLA

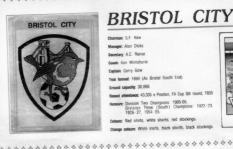

BRISTOL CITY

ASHTO

BRISTOL CITY

Chairman: S.F. Kew
Manager: Alan Dicks
Secretary: A.E. Rance
Coach: Ken Wimshurst
Captain: Garry Gow
Year formed: 1894 (As Bristol South End)
Ground capacity: 30,868
Record attendance: 43,335 v Preston, FA Cup 5th round, 1935
Honours: Division Two Champions: 1905-06.
Division Three (South) Champions: 1922-23,
1926-27, 1954-55.
Colours: Red shirts, white shorts, red stockings.
Change colours: White shirts, black shorts, black stockings.

BRISTOL CI

FOOTBALL LEAGUE FIRST DIVISION

ALAN DICKS — BRISTOL CITY Manager

Enjoyed a fine career as a midfield player with Millwall, Chelsea, Southend and Coventry before taking over the managerial reins at Ashton Gate in October 1967. Took City into the First Division in 1976. Made City's youngest captain. Made his debut against Aston Villa in May 1968, and has since clocked up over 300 League appearances for his local team.

JOHN SHAW — BRISTOL CITY

Goalkeeper. Born Stirling. Ht.6.1.Wt.13.7. Age 24. Signed on originally for Leeds, but could not make the first team, and moved to Bristol City in May 1974 on a free transfer. Made his League debut against Birmingham in October 1976, and has been regular first choice 'keeper ever since.

Defender. Born Glasgow. 34. Started with Celtic the first team there, a Morton. Signed by C 1971 and has since over 300 League ap Can also play effecti

GEOFF MERRICK — BRISTOL CITY

Defender. Born Bristol. Ht.5.9.Wt.11.0. Age 28. Schoolboy international who joined City from school and at only 20 became the Football League's youngest captain. Made his debut against Aston Villa in May 1968, and has clocked up over 300 League appearances for his local team.

DAVID RODGERS — BRISTOL CITY

Defender. Born Bristol. Ht.6.1%. Wt.13.2. Age 27. Another local schoolboy international and son of ex-City striker Arnold Rodgers. Made his debut in 1971, and despite being dogged by injuries, now has over 130 League appearances behind him. Plays in the centre-half position.

Midfield. Born Bristo A former schoolboy in pro with City in Se his League debut in Carlisle. Now, with pearances behind hi serving player.

sticker. Room for the second division sides and the Scottish Premier League, too.

Panini largely resisted the old FKS fallback of crude recolouring if they didn't have a photo of the player in correct kit – although Tony Towers of Birmingham City and Manchester United's Jimmy Greenhoff both had paint jobs.

There was hardly a corner of the school playground where a swap deal wasn't going down as the new craze took a vice-like grip. By the time we'd completed our sets we could hardly wait for 1979 to come round, so we could do it all again.

Panini delivered the goods every year, rarely deviating from the head-and-shoulders format, except for 1983 when the players appeared full length, catching out

a bootless Bob Latchford.

Panini were the undisputed sticker kings throughout the '80s and up to 1991 when they produced their most expansive album ever with a whopping 553 stickers, plus a few extras. But things were about to change...

With the Premier League launch imminent, licensing fees were hotting up and Panini's 'English Football 1992' was a stripped-down effort of 276 match-action stickers reminicent of the FKS days. It was under the banner of the PFA, nominally 'The Offical Players' Collection'.

As documented in Greg Lansdowne's *Stuck on You*, a group of former Panini employees had set up Merlin Publishing, much to the displeasure of their former boss, Robert Maxwell. They had the ear of David Dein at Arsenal, and a potent blend of raw enthusiasm and just enough cash saw them unexpectedly scoop the Premier League sticker rights.

Although they still had the iconic World Cup albums, and secured a Football League deal, Panini's golden age covering top-flight football was over.

COVENTRY
HUTCHINSON

COVENTRY
HUNDLEY

DERBY COUNTY
PRIOCH

Looney Toon: It's Bob Moncur at Whitley Bay, honest pet.

EVERTON
EVERTON

LEICESTER CITY
CLOVER

DERBY COUNTY
DANS

The Full Monty

Intrigued by our eccentric collection of Monty Gum's 'Football Now' cards, and their uncanny ability to get players' names *very nearly* right, we referenced their entry on the world's number one web resource covering cards and stickers of the '60s and '70s. It turns out the company was Dutch, and produced football cards from the '50s through to the '90s.

"Unnumbered, poor quality cards on a cheap card with plain grey backs," judges Nigel Mercer in his eponymous Webspace. "The quality control on the player and team names is also very suspect, with one card mentioning both the player and team name as 'Everton' (actually Terry Darracott)."

But that's not to say that Nigel doesn't love the cards to bits. He even goes and tracks down Hannah's of Johnstone, the distribution company mentioned on the Monty's packaging. Long-lost secrets are unearthed about curiously collectable football, Kojak and Space 1999 sets – and important questions raised regarding the shocking absence of gum in Monty Gum packets.

Dandy from Denmark

In terms of longevity, breadth of subject matter (lots of pop, flags and animals) and hugely desirable dips in football card quality, Dandy Gum could be described, not unkindly, as Denmark's own operator in the Monty Gum niche.

Once you've seen these splendid approximations of 'Football Kits of the World' (that's Man United, Man City, Newcastle…) you'll need to add your club's card to your collection. Marvel at the huge set – at the hundreds of mates, students and vagrants roped in to stand in a featureless Danish field and struggle to make believe.

badly drawn boy

Pop Art: BAB's best were masterpieces of the naive folk style.

The Sticker Detective

For decades, Nigel Mercer fretted over the origins of the BAB 'Pictorial Map of Soccer' which illuminated his '70s childhood along with the basic but now famously collectable stickers the shadowy company produced.

In the pages of *Got, Not Got*, we recounted his detective work, the sticker equivalent of an episode of *Columbo*, involving Clive Sinclair and a backstreet publishing company that still survives in Shepherds Bush.

We're now chuffed to update you with Nigel's discovery of a second company involved in the printing of small, sticky shields featuring iffy images of footballers and imaginatively coloured versions of club badges! As it turns out, any vinyl stickers among the priceless treasures wasted on your PE bag were probably produced not by BAB but by the Leeds company, Northern Trancessories.

So now you know, you can sleep peacefully in your bed at night.

Unless, of course, you can recall visiting your corner shop and seeing a BAB counter display like this one – with the one near-priceless sticker, totally forgotten until last year. Yours for a penny.

"Can I have 36 of your Alun Evanses, please, Mr Sherrard?"

Dereliction Chic: One of the lesser-known views of good old White Hart Lane.

Maxwell: Because Ján Ludvík Hyman Binyamin Hoch didn't fit in the box.

happy motoring!

Go! with Got, Not Got

Some of the most popular car-based collectables were designed to dangle distractingly from your rear-view mirror.

Throughout the final decades of the 20th century there were countless variations on the mini kit in-car shrine – some officially licensed and others not; some laudably accurate in their kit detail and others more... impressionistic.

Some of the less reputable types also boasted the dubious bonus of an air-freshener, which were great if you really wanted your motor's natural aroma of overflowing ashtrays to be replaced with the scent of fresh mountain pine (aka toilet cleaner).

Interestingly, it was kit manufacturers Bukta behind the 'Be-Be' mini-kits, a fact that escaped most collectors' notice. But, in turn, Bukta's marketing department had taken their eye off the ball if they really imagined many fans would collect more than one of the set.

The threat of vandalism had, by the '70s, largely put paid to the football club car grille badge. It took a brave fan indeed to venture out of their hometown with a club badge proudly on display next to their RAC plaque. Vintage examples for the smaller clubs, especially, are now highly prized.

Talking of tactically keeping a low profile, pity the poor pro of our golden age – with his name and club emblazoned on his sponsor car door in a mixture of criminal hand-painted fonts. The Baby Bentley set really don't know they're born, do they?

The end of your journey to Goodison is in sight – powered by 4-Star Cleveland, sustained by two small plastic busts.

Petrol Freebies

It's been one of the big personal bonuses of spending so long piecing together this cataloguish cornucopia of collectables. Not since they came out in 1971 had I held in my hand a Big League 'Star of the '70s' figurine. They've been a holy grail item (along with those little plastic TV slide viewers) for decades, difficult to even look up as I couldn't remember the issuer, and 'little gold footballers' doesn't

hit the jackpot on eBay or Google. It turns out they weren't from Fina or Cleveland but from Total. This superb set on its original display stand wouldn't be worth much more if the figures were real gold.

Meanwhile, it *was* Cleveland stations offering Joe Mercer's GB Soccer Squad in 1971. The neat little busts are quite common today. Again, it's the slotted display stand of classy black and gold plastic that's really hard to find.

From the same era, the two sets of Esso football coins really caught everybody's attention, and passed right into popular culture. For years throughout the '80s we used to hark back to when Esso gave us free gifts instead of just ripping us off to to the tune of 40p per litre.

And then, out of the blue, a new generation got the chance to collect another wonderful set for Italia 90, this time including both England and Scotland players.

FOOTBALL TRIPS

SATURDAY 7TH MAY, 1983

Oldham Athletic v Leicester City
At Boundary Park. Kick-off 15.00 hours

Excursion to
OLDHAM WERNETH

Return Fare : £4.50

NO HALF FARES

Outward			Return
10.40 dep. Kettering	arr. 20.47
10.54 dep. Market Harborough	arr. 20.33
11.12 dep. Leicester	arr. 20.10
11.27 dep. Loughborough	arr. 19.54
14.09 arr. Oldham Werneth	dep. 17.30

Accommodation limited – Book in advance
Passengers will be issued with special tickets which are only valid
for travel by this service.

The Board do not undertake to refund fares or other charges in
the event of cancellation of this match. No Alcohol allowed on
this service.

All fares and facilities shown are subject to alteration or
cancellation

British Rail

BR35157/72

Class Ticket type
2ND FOOTEX 2968 1402
Date 03MAY88 Number 01317
From
MANCHESTER PIC
To
Watford Jcn.
via Special Train £10.00M
1402
British Rail Outward

Class
2ND FOOTEX 2968 1536
Date 12FEBY84Q Number 47441
From
MANCHESTER PIC £8.00M
Luton 1536
via Special Train
British Rail Outward

Day return 2nd
F.A. Cup Semi-Final
Leicester City v Tottenham
SAT. 3rd APRIL 1982
Loughborough, Leicester
to
WITTON and back
For conditions see over (M) 1047

Day return 2nd
SAT 31 JAN 1981
Kettering, Market Harborough,
Leicester, Loughborough,
to
LIVERPOOL
(Lime Street) and back
For conditions see over (M) 1047

I only asked,
'How much is it
to Oldham?' and
got my ticket
punched.

2nd - DAY
"EXPLORE BRITAIN
LONDON (ST
AND B PANCRAS) BACK
3 MAY 1980
For condit... see over

Did you arrive by car today?

... next time save petrol,
avoid the aggro and travel to the
Goldstone by train. Park your car
at your local station and buy
an Awayday ticket to Hove.

Some examples of Awayday return fares
to Hove:

Shoreham 55p	Eastbourne £2.00
Worthing 95p	Three Bridges £1.79
Littlehampton £1.63	Haywards Heath £1.15
Lewes 95p	Burgess Hill 95p
Polegate £1.79	

Southern

fully trained

61662
MANCHESTER UNITED

ST. ANDREWS
VILLA PARK
THE HAWTHORNS
SPECIAL
FOOTBALL
SPECIAL
RACES
CITY
SANDON RD. 6
PERRY COMMON 5
(COURT LANE)
PERRY COMMON
PORTLAND RD. 7
QUINTON 9
INNER CIRCLE 8
HOCKLEY
FIVE WAYS
SALTLEY
ASTON CROSS
SPRING HILL
(MONUMENT RD.)

FOOTBALL GROUND
619
KVH 219

Football Special: All aboard for the Blues, the Villa or the Baggies.

Transports of Delight

Nothing excites a bloke quite as much as an outdated mode of transport. Any journey in the past can seem supremely romantic, looking back on events distorted by warm, fuzzy memories of vintage rolling stock, overpriced BR sandwiches and cans of Skol. And then arriving somewhere – *anywhere* – in yer actual, sunny 1983. Yes, even Oldham.

Throw in the double whammy of a rose-tinted day on a Football Special, ideally under heavy police guard, and fans will go to surprising lengths to recreate their perfect away day.

Corgi Toy coaches and model trains. Travel itineraries, domestic or Continental. Ticket collections expanded to include those issued on trains, planes and coaches as well as at the turnstiles. They can all help recall the atmosphere of bygone glories and pilgrimages, all the better if they happened to be aboard the legendary disco carriage on the *League Liner* train.

It isn't just the away experience but also the old, familiar trip to home matches that's now subject to eBaymania. Vintage football bus tickets, sections of destination blinds and even club parking passes are all on the up-and-up.

What might seem odd to some is the market for ephemera covering historical trips and games where the collector wasn't even present.

visit SPOTLAND!

Rochdale, Here We Come

Our thanks go out to Mark Wilbraham, editor of Rochdale AFC's programme, *The Voice of Spotland*, for getting in touch with these hugely atmospheric images of home. They represent an example of our very favourite kind of football awayday, not just a trip in space but also in time.

Ever since they sold off and built a housing estate on Kettering Town's Rockingham Road ground, we've been pining for the old-school 'matchday experience' that involved standing up, cavernous mismatched stands and a real-ale bar with a window out on to the pitch, approximately 10 feet from the touchline.

1 – With all due respect to modern Premier League stadia, there have never been 60 different food and drink outlets at Spotland, and we think it's probably just as

well. On the other hand, they're really missing out on a muckheap round the back of the Main Stand at Spurs' new stadium.

2 – We miss the homely feel of grounds with a big welcome in the car park and a view from the stands of the surrounding town, or at least an occasional tree. Spotland's got the lot.

3 – Taking a break from mending the perimeter wall are John Wood, Brian Clough (no, not that one), Marion Wood, unknown, Geoff Mawdsley, Steve Bonynge behind

Brian Gee, and Colin Smith.

4 – Our action shot shows Dale skipper Brian Taylor and mascots v Hull in an FA Cup first round match in November 1981, ably assisted by commercial manager Brian Johnson in his state-of-art car coat. The game ended 2-2, the bigtime rivals from Yorkshire only edging the tie after two replays.

Our favourite Rochdale fact: In the League since 1921, the club had never won a game in London before they beat Barnet 4-0 away in October 1995.

Around and About

Let's dive back into the halcyon days of away travel, wilfully ignore all the blatant negatives such as hooliganism and dilapidation, and try to focus our dewy eyes on a few of the vast, ramshackle arenas that were doomed to conversion and/or execution.

1 – The East Stand at Chelsea was built in 1974, replacing the Leitch original. A magnificently brutal three-tier monstrosity, it survives in part today.

2 – The Shed, all rickety and skew-whiff on the adjoining south side of Stamford Bridge, was demolished in 1994 when the capacity was reduced to 34,000.

3 – You've seen enough pictures of the church in the corner at Goodison Park. For balance, here's the stairwell extension on the end of the Bullens Road side.

4 – The Art Deco facade of the East Stand at Highbury, which contained the awe-inspiring marble entrance hall, the bust of

Herbert Chapman and Arsenal loco nameplate. Now undead, a novelty block of posh flats.

5 – Boundary Park, Oldham, atop its bleak and blustery hill in the late '80s.

6 – The old South Stand at Blackpool (you guessed) posing behind our photographer-guide, Karl Hanssens, who we have to thank for all these glimpses into the Lost World.

7 – The Holte End at Villa Park, which used to hold 22,600 before

the advent of all-seater stadia. At this time, in the late '80s, it could claim bragging rights to be the biggest Kop in the country.

8 – The Park Lane End at Tottenham, unusual in that the stand gradually gets further from the pitch, following the line of the road behind. The seam in the roof marks the departure point.

9 – The Grand Stand at Preston North End's Deepdale. Built in 1906 in anticipation of another period of success, if not invincibility. It remained a stately sight, from the inside, at least, until its demolition in 1995.

10 – The Stretford End – 'a sound trap of red and white aggression', wrote Simon Inglis in 1983. 'For sheer partisan noise and atmosphere, there is not a ground in England to match Old Trafford.'

11 – And the Scoreboard End, complete with the Munich Clock and plaque commemorating the victims of the 1958 Air Disaster.

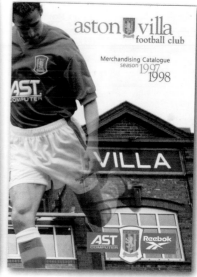

shop 'til you drop

Welcome to the Meagrestore

How exciting it used to be to pop into the club's corner shop on Saturday lunchtime for a rosette, a pennant, a team photo or genuine silky scarf. Okay, we'll settle for an enamel badge. There were rarely football kits on sale; they were to be found at the sports outfitters in the middle of town.

Of course, times swiftly changed. But in comparison to today's big-brand retail outlets, football's first-gen fairly-superstores were really rather modest affairs.

1 – This fan was stopped right in his tracks by the motherlode of Spurs stuff. He'll be through that turnstile in a jiffy, thrilled to bits by his plastic Christmas holdall.

2 – Inside the pioneering club shop at Leeds United, home of the sock-tag and the Kevin Hird rosette. The first time I ever saw a section of the crowd wearing replica shirts was at Elland Road in 1987/88. Back then, only kiddies wore football shirts when they weren't actually playing or at a school PE lesson.

4

★

OZZIE OWL says...
I have three shops open this week . . .
one next to the Pools Office, one at
Spion Kop and one at Leppings Lane
end. Bags of things for you to buy . . .
all at bargain prices . . .
Get your boater now !

★

6

5

7

3 – United did a good job of disguising their Mk1 Megastore as a holiday chalet. In fairness, it was Tardis-like. The same size as a police box. But our photo contributor, Karl, was still well impressed.

4 – 'Welcome Frannie!' New chairman, loo-roll magnate F. Lee, has just taken over at Maine Road and instantly ordered a panic sale.

5 – The Liverpool FC Souvenir Shop did well to keep trade to an absolute minimum on matchday. Not only was the main display window smaller than the front window of an average semi, they also made things tricky for fans by removing the outside door.

6 – Ozzie Owl was way ahead of the curve. No, not with his straw

boaters but with his precedent to the pop-up shops now so common on our impoverished high streets.

7 – It's the club shop at Wivenhoe Town of the Eastern Counties League Division One South. The Dragons may be a few decades off the pace, but check the precedents and you can tell big things are coming to Broad Lane.

You Don't See That So Much Now

At first glance, there's nothing so remarkable about these forgotten images of a low-key match in the early '70s; but the longer we stared into the pixels, the more mystery and wonderment we unearthed.

For starters, it was far from clear who was playing. Palace are at home, but they're wearing a change kit against a team who might be South American tourists? A pre-season friendly? The more you see, the less familiar everything seems to become.

1 – The wall. Still available at many grounds, but anyone caught perched on a 7-foot vantage point would now likely be ejected and shot for their own safety.

2 – The floodlight pylon. Correctly positioned mid terrace, a strutted steel pylon could offer many thrilling variations of the restricted view.

3 – Supporters' Club bar at the back of the terrace. Cheers!

4 – Walk Don't Run. No pushing, no surging, no running, no shouting, no bombing, no petting.

5 – Crush barriers.

6 – Local advertising hoardings.

7 – Bobbies ignoring the match and chatting about a recent angling trip.

8 – Longhairs, ditto.

9 – Foreign team looking a bit clueless. You don't see so many crack exotic sides milling aimlessly around the midfield these days, let alone wearing black boots.

10 – A view out of the ground, offering a sense of time, place and perspective up Whitehorse Lane.

11 – Socks round ankles. Another Health & Safety no-no nowadays. Steve Kember carded.

Thanks to Pete Hurn who finally identified the match: Crystal Palace v Maccabi Nathanya, on 6th August 1971.

"It was 8-1," added Pete Fuell via Twitter. "I'm there in the White-horse End. We ran on the pitch and mobbed their goalscorer!"

Beloved of Villa fan Inglis, the beautiful red-brick Trinity Road Stand was tragically demolished in 2000.

SIMON INGLIS
FOOTBALL GROUNDS OF BRITAIN
MAJOR NEW EDITION

SIMON INGLIS
The Football Grounds of Europe

THE FOOTBALL GROUNDS OF ENGLAND AND WALES
SIMON INGLIS
Published in association with The Football League and The National Dairy Council

Ground Zero

First published in 1983 as *The Football Grounds of England and Wales*, Simon Inglis's odyssey captured the unique atmosphere and sometimes battered beauty of every club's home at a crucial time, immediately before they changed radically or beyond recognition. Inglis's architectural expertise was worn easily, and his dismay at many dangerous, crumbling structures would often give way to a warm-hearted overview.

"There ought to be tours from the promenade taking visitors to Bloomfield Road, if only to see the West Stand," he wrote of Blackpool. "It is the quintessential British football grandstand, impossible to recreate in concrete and steel. How long it will survive perhaps only Blackpool's famous

fortune tellers can say."

To reread it today is to risk an overdose of retrospective irony, if not a crippling sense of loss:

"Of course it is not perfect, but then Oxford is full of unsuitable buildings, and maybe, just maybe, United would lose their heart and soul if they left this cloistered quadrangle for some brave new world out on the ring road."

Darlington's Feethams is "the sort of ground where one sees the odd squirrel scooting across the terraces, evoking memories of how football and football grounds once were... simply an open space where sporting young men turned out for the love of the game."

If you're the kind of day tripper that enjoys following around out-

of-date guidebooks (it can't just be us?), then there are still elusive pleasures to be had.

Aberdeen's ancestral seat is "a barrier against the sea; a place to huddle", and is a rarity within these pages in that it remains so, it's character having survived the construction of a new stand only 500 yards from the North Sea.

But, for now, we're tootling off to Bournemouth for the weekend, hoping for small-scale pleasures: "A football ground amid the lace curtains, perms and poodles seems about as inappropriate as a beer glass at a cocktail party. Dean Court makes one wish rather wish there were more grounds like this, tucked in among the lobelias and leaf-strewn paths."

Fulham

The Lost Cottagers

It gives us a real thrill to think that there'll be plenty of Fulham fans who have never seen this set of stickers from the super-rare FKS album of 1967/68.

As a trial version of the first album to be distributed nationwide the following season, many of the 330 stickers remained the same. But sadly Fulham were relegated and so missed out on their place in the spotlight. Until now.

Here's the legendary Johnny Haynes, World Cup winner George Cohen and Allan Clarke before his British record transfer

to Leicester. It's a double pleasure to share the album page because Nigel Mercer, card aficionado, is himself a Fulham fan.

Hibernian

Infamy, Infamy

Back in 1977/78 Hibs made history as the first British League club to wear sponsored shirts, sporting an advert for their shirt manufacturers, Bukta. It was a great period for nationwide column inches for the Edinburgh club, as George

Best was soon to blow into town at the invitation of chairman Tom Hart.

Best signed a £2,000-per-match contract and made his

debut at St Mirren's Love Street in November 1979.

In all, Best was with the club for 325 days, pulling on the infamous green Bukta shirt 22 times and scoring three goals.

Heart of Midlothian

Mixed Memories

After Ajax won the European Cup in 1971 and '72, Hearts decided to follow suit stylistically with one

the season held few golden memories for the struggling

DONALD FORD

of their most popular home shirts ever. But while the Dutch masters triumphed again in 1972/73,

Jambos, who lost 0-7 at home to Hibs. Now retro designs are all the rage, the beautiful shirt could surely be considered for a comeback – a natural winner, especially paired with a traditional heart badge?

Huddersfield Town

Like a Terrier

Whether you're a Terriers fan or not, Roger Pashby's Huddersfield Town Collection website is a splendid place to while away a reflective half-hour. Roger started out with football cards but now he's got pretty much everything HTFC in

his virtual museum.

Among our favourite items were this fearsome badge from a player's shirt in the second-from-last glory era – could it have been Frank Worthington's? – and a thoughtful-looking West Yorkshire terrier money box from the same era.

Ipswich Town

Men of Bronze

Erected in 2000 shortly after his death, the statue of Sir Alf Ramsey at Portman Road captures something of the manager's nonchalant poise. In charge from 1955, Sir Alf led Town to the First Division championship in 1961/62 before moving on to England in '63. And you-know-what.

The 2002 statue of Sir Bobby was in place seven years before his passing. Again, sculptor Sean Hedges-Quinn successfully got to the essence of the man, his energy and humour. Town manager from 1969-82, Sir Bobby brought home the 1978 FA Cup and 1981 UEFA Cup. Two must-have adornments for every mantelpiece in Ipswich. The miniature versions, that is...

Sir ALFRED RAMSEY 1920 ~ 1999

Leeds United

Long, Hot Summer

With the close-season over at last, the superstars of Super Leeds reconvene for the endless promise of 1976/77. No more lazing with the family on Spanish beaches. From here on in, it's all hard work and a strict diet.

Best of all, there's a fabulous new kit from Admiral Sportswear. Tony Currie, Terry Yorath, Gordon McQueen, David 'Daisy' McNiven – what great names – all look as excited as the kids that would soon be modelling the miniature versions.

A Splash of Colour

For a bricks-and-mortar illustration of civilisation in a downward spiral, take a walk down Long Street in Wigston, on the outskirts of Leicester.

There stands a dilapidated old factory, boarded up and with half the roof missing after a fire. This was once Admiral HQ, where the air buzzed with the sound of sewing machines, and rows of ladies applied countless little yellow logos to shirts, shorts, socks and tracky tops.

Once Cook & Hurst Ltd decided that the future was in football kits rather than underpants, a revolution in football branding began. Chairman Bert Patrick wanted to create more distinctive kits than the plain generic strips available at the time, giving clubs ownership of their look.

Leeds United were the first, their yellow away kit sporting blue and white stripes down the sleeves, then England, with essentially the same design. Manchester United were next, then Coventry City and Wales with their tramlines down the front of shirts and shorts, before the whole thing blossomed into a riot of colour like wildflowers in a meadow.

If you'd ever wondered who was

Admiral Sportswear:
More tramlines than a
pre-war city centre.

responsible for classics like the West Ham chevrons or Norwich's rhapsody in yellow and green, the joyous 2016 documentary *Get Shirty* revealed that it was a young girl straight out of art college.

"I was not a football fan at all but, yes, you did try to come up with something different." Lindsay Jelley's lack of football knowledge was what allowed her to introduce such a flamboyant touch to football strips from Aberdeen to Southampton. "I actually didn't know what had come before. I was interested in colours and shapes and all these different things, so as long as they came to me and said, 'Lindsay we need something in these colours,' away I went, I loved it." And we loved them too, so thanks Lindsay.

Sadly, Admiral became victims of their own success when other brands with more financial muscle decided they wanted a slice of the replica kit business they'd created. That's when the difficult transition from small firm to global business saw them stutter financially and enter receivership.

In an ideal world, one run by 50-something football fans with a retro obsession, that burnt out factory on Long Street would now be the Admiral Museum.

From Manchester with Love

While Umbro had been producing wonderfully stylish football kits for many decades, their branding was always hidden from view. But in the summer of 1976 the diamonds were finally unearthed...

Working as a salesman for Stockport sportswear firm Bukta in the 1920s left a teenage Harold Humphreys feeling that this wasn't the route to success. So he teamed up with sibling Wallace to form Humphreys Brothers Ltd – and was later unsuccessfully sued by his former employers, and now rivals, for copyright infringement in the Umbro catalogue.

After a decade of gradual growth Umbro kitted out Manchester City for the 1934 FA Cup final, and never looked back. Many landmark football moments of the 20th century were achieved with an Umbro diamond sewn into the collar, Blackpool's FA Cup win in 1953, Tottenham's Double in 1961, England's 1966 World Cup triumph, Celtic's 1967 European Cup triumph. But not until the early '70s did the logo become visible. It first appeared on Leeds and Sunderland shirts in the 1973 FA Cup final, and the following season Liverpool, Sheffield Utd and Derby all followed suit.

By 1974/75 this had become the norm with a new double diamond logo on Manchester City's shirts and a text version worn by Wolves.

Possibly prodded into action by Admiral's innovative new approach to branding, Umbro launched a new range for the 1976/77 season with a mouth-watering advert in *Shoot!* – "It's going to be a sparkling season... just look at those diamonds!"

Derby, Everton, Bristol City, Scotland, Blackpool and Manchester City all wore kits with diamond taping down the sleeves and shorts. While Arsenal and Liverpool stuck with the plainer tradition, plenty more clubs joined the party the following season

diamonds are forever

Not content with kitting out half of the Football League, Umbro also dressed the Scouts.

when an updated double diamond taping was introduced including Bolton, Chelsea, West Brom, Wolves, Cardiff, Stoke, Hearts, Morton, Partick Thistle...

It was a simple and elegant template, from the dawn of kit design, though things were to get much more complicated in the years to come.

UMBRO · OFFICIAL **NEW STYLE SCOUTWEAR**

OFFICIALLY APPROVED BY THE SCOUT ASSOCIATION

1968

Presented by UMBRO

Bobby Dassler

There were many parallels in the histories of Adidas and Umbro. In the austere aftermath of the Great War, Adi Dassler utilised his mother's laundry shed in Herzogenaurach to start his sports footwear business, while Harold Humphreys was working out of a box room in his mother's pub in Mobberley.

After they'd both battled their way to the top of their respective fields the two companies struck up a deal in 1961. Umbro would be the sole distributor of Adidas footwear in the UK, and the German firm would stay out of the kit market.

This arrangement, based on the friendship between the two patriarchs, would not survive their passing. As it became obvious that the replica kit market was going to make big bucks, Adidas wanted a slice. They kitted out QPR for the 1976/77 season and then expanded their roster for 1977/78, adding Birmingham City, Middlesbrough, Ipswich Town and Nottingham Forest. They chose wisely, ending the season with a clean sweep of the FA Cup (Ipswich), the League title and League Cup (Forest).

The demise of Admiral led to the

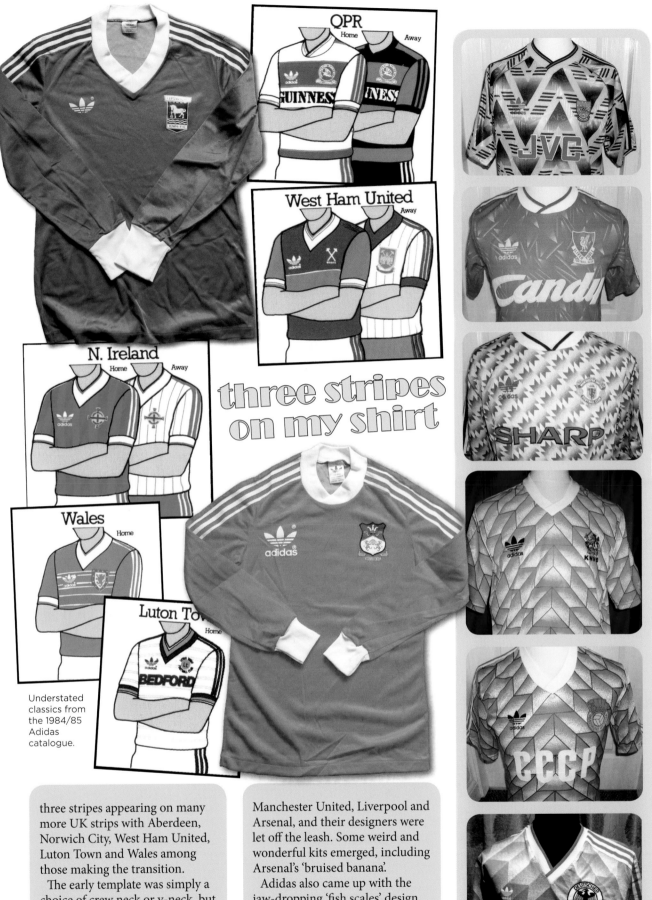

QPR
Home · Away
GUINNESS

West Ham United
Away

N. Ireland
Home · Away

Wales
Home

Luton Town
Home
BEDFORD

Understated classics from the 1984/85 Adidas catalogue.

three stripes on my shirt

JVC

Candy

SHARP

KNVB

CCCP

DEUTSCHER FUSSBALL-BUND

three stripes appearing on many more UK strips with Aberdeen, Norwich City, West Ham United, Luton Town and Wales among those making the transition.

The early template was simply a choice of crew neck or v-neck, but Adidas soon came up with some classily designed strips using pin-stripes and then shadow weave.

By the late '80s Adidas fully concentrated on the big three of

Manchester United, Liverpool and Arsenal, and their designers were let off the leash. Some weird and wonderful kits emerged, including Arsenal's 'bruised banana'.

Adidas also came up with the jaw-dropping 'fish scales' design for Euro 88 – officially known as the 'Ipswich' template. Though it never made it to these shores, this design regularly comes close to the top of all-time great kits polls.

SHAW CARPETS

Love, Hate, Love to Hate

Here's a selection of 'adventurous' kits made by small manufacturers that always spurred oppo fans to take the mickey, but which have since become prized items among fans and collectors.

Barnsley's infamous 'cowboy' shirt was made by Paul Trevillion's Beaver International. It crops up regularly in bad kit features, so aficionados of tasteful kit assume it's unpopular at Oakwell. However, Tykes fan Matthew Lumb informed us that they're so sought after that a local company have brought out a reproduction.

Brighton's pink NOBO away shirt of 1989-91 was another debatable classic, produced by the long-defunct Sports Express and now worth over £200! Ditto Villa's Henson shirt of 1985-87, which looked like a DIY effort following on from the classy Le Coq kit. But fans love it, along with Norwich's notorious Ribero 'egg and cress' kit, which holds fond memories of a win over Bayern Munich.

When Avec shattered Sheffield United's stripes into diamonds in 1995/96, you might think the Blades would have protested at such a break with Yorkshire tradition. But, no. Likewise Super League's garish Plymouth effort of 1996-98, Boro's Skill-crafted bodge of '87/88 and Carlisle's 1995-97 Red Fox 'deckchair' effort in Eddie Stobart livery. All fondly remembered by the fans. They may be dog's dinners, but they're *our* dog's dinners.

THE ADIDAS HISTORY OF SOCCER

adidas

boxing clever

umbro
INTERNATIONAL

CODE 2152/85

CHELSEA (HOME)

Umbroset for Boys. Not forgetting girls, grown men, etc.

Soccer Smashes Sopranos

Not a lot of people know that football beat TV to the box-set concept, hands down. By the time the BBC and ITV had the hot idea of marketing their old repeats on VHS video, in slipboxes the size of a suitcase, the football kit box set was at least 20 years old.

Umbro were the first company to offer a complete football kit of matching shirt, shorts and socks in a handy all-in-one package.

Single-handedly, they kicked off the replica kit industry aimed primarily at 5-12 year-olds, as early as 1959. Umbro used an image of Matt Busby in the ad campaign and on the box of the ground-breaking product, shortly to be branded as the Umbroset.

In 1964, the more dynamic figure of Denis Law became the figurehead. As the marketing of football evolved in the later '60s he was the embodiment of the hero we could all emulate by slipping into a miniature version of his kit.

Tribal lines were not yet drawn to prevent Law flogging his own United kit alongside that of seven other English clubs, three Scottish, and the England international kit.

The flaw in the market was the generic nature of the '60s kits. There was nothing to stop other companies producing plain red shirts with a white collar. And this was a challenge that was taken up by contenders Admiral and Adidas with a little more gusto than the comfortable market leader.

97

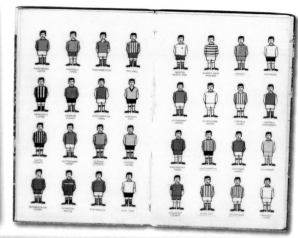

League Division 1

League Division 3

Scottish League Division 1

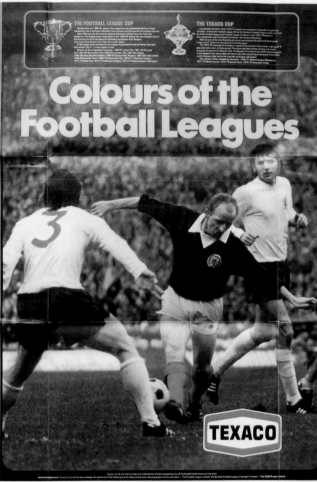

Colours of the Football Leagues

THE FOOTBALL LEAGUE CUP

THE TEXACO CUP

TEXACO

League Division 2

League Division 4

Scottish League Division 2

All My Colours

There must have been a time tens of thousands of years ago when carefully logging, cataloguing and memorising colours was of vital importance to man's survival. Long buried beneath the surface of our consciousness, it's a vestigial trait – though we'd really prefer to think of it as quite a talent – that still surfaces today whenever we start to notice and compare the minutiae of different football uniforms. Once it was probably trees and fruit we considered

from the safety of our man caves. Then train livery, postage stamps, Pokémon cards...

I only wish my online calendar had a cool, calming kit section like *The Legible Soccer Diary* from '66.

Ooh, look at that Bradford City, that exotic Carlisle and Killie on the Texaco poster from 1974/75.

And then there's our uncut sheet of Tower Press transfers, with the 1965/66 Arsenal kit that seemed to upset the natural order. But things turn out okay thanks to Plymouth, resplendent in all green.

LEAGUE CLUBS: COLOUR GUIDE

Norwich City   Notts County

Nottingham Forest   Oldham Athletic   Orient

Oxford United   Peterborough United

Launched with no marketing budget, word of mouth made Fingersaves a hit.

Gloved Up

An inviting peek into Rob Stokes' collection of goalkeeping memorabilia which includes 700+ vintage mitts, stars of *Glove Story*. They range from early woollens via '70s Adidas with 'table-tennis bat' grips, up to the iconic shot-stoppers of the '90s:

1 – Uhlsport 036, 1989. Worn by Erik Thorstvedt, John Burridge, Ian Walker, Jim Leighton. And Peter Shilton, reaching in vain for German penalties at the 1990 World Cup semi-final.

2 – Reusch Peter Schmeichel, 1991. Long-term favourites for the Great Dane. Lifted countless PL trophies and FA Cups, though UEFA restrictions on logo size and number forced a change for the 1999 Champions League final.

3 – Umbro Grobbelaar Premier, 1991. The first time a cartoon keeper ever appeared on the index finger of a pair of gloves.

4 – Adidas Fingersave, 1994. Shaka Hislop, Shay Given and Steve Ogrizovic were among those who dived in to wear these revolutionary gloves with spines running down the fingers. 'Save the finger' and 'save the shot'...

What must Gordon Banks must have thought of these gloves' high technology, having worn gardening gloves in the 1966 World Cup final. And no psychedelic shirts back in his day!

Sensational POWER-POINTS
These fantastic new boots make winning football easy!

TUFSPIN
The revolutionary new football boot we've all been waiting for.

Tufspin by **hummel** The best in boots.

If you can't score in these, **retire.**

The new adidas Predator football boot approved by FIFA.
Power, swerve and control in a lighter form.
Even more of a devastating touch.
Even less room for excu—

adidas

100% legal
0% fair.

PREDATOR adidas

"Everyone kept asking me, 'What are they?'" – John Collins of Celtic

THE MAN—THE BOOT—THE BALL

Jimmy Greaves
WEARS and WEARS ONLY
ZEPHYR FOOTBALL BOOTS

Zephyr Football Boots and Zephyr Footballs make a perfect combination.

ZEPHYR FOOTBALLS have been used this season for the AMATEUR CUP FINAL at WEMBLEY
BOYS' INTERNATIONAL
England v Germany at NORTHAMPTON
YOUTHS' INTERNATIONAL
England v Germany at WEMBLEY
obtainable from all leading Sports Outfitters

LAWRENCE SPORTS DISTRIBUTORS LTD.
STANWICK · WELLINGBOROUGH   Telephone RAUNDS 46

❶

Kinky Boots

There was never a boot more perfectly Swinging '60s than the Zephyr LSD. Touted by Jimmy Greaves as well as the Beatles, it came in any colour so long as it was black or shimmery rainbow.

The Hummel Tufspin was groovy, too. White-hot plastic. Rotating studs that enabled you to spin on the spot. Just the job so long as you never wanted to run straight ahead, with ankles intact.

Meanwhile, the genius of Power Points was the sticky numbered patches that helpfully renamed your instep, the outside of your foot and heel '1', '2' and '3' respectively. Pure gimmick heaven.

Enter the Predator

Back in 1992 former Liverpool star Craig Johnston signed a deal with Adidas for the manufacturing and marketing of the Predator football boot, with all-new rubber ribbing to assist in swerving the ball. After 300 prototypes in four years, the Adidas Predator was finally launched in May 1994, with the help of Marcel Desailly and Celtic's John Collins – the first player to wear the boot in Britain.

1 – The groundbreaking Predator and its original packaging, along with a dramatic print ad from the time of the launch. The futuristic sci-fi look really caught the imagination, along with the edgy

'100% legal, 0% fair' ad campaign. Thanks to Predator supercollector Hinson Chung (@thepredatorpro on Instagram) for all these boots and collectables, especially the promo T-shirt, caps and backpack, which are impossibly rare.

2 – The second-gen Predator Rapier of 1995 was the first evolution with a fold-over tongue, available in different colours.

3 – The Predator Touch featured a red fold-over tongue, an enlarged striking zone and Traxion outsole. Think Gazza's goal for England v Scotland at Euro 96, and Beckham scoring from the halfway line.

4 – The Predator Accelerator, quite possibly the most famous Predator ever, introduced for the 1998 World Cup in France. Think Zinédine Zidane and his semi-transparent outsoles.

5 – The holy grail for many collectors is the Adidas Predator Accelerator colourway.

6 – Adidas Predator Precision. The screw-in magnesium Traxion system now enabled players to customise their boots...

7 – ...also in futuristic silver.

8 – We asked Hinson to pick out his prize boots in this initial 1994-2000 window, and he opted for his Predator Precision Platinum Edition, somewhere beyond rare as they were limited to only 333 pairs in the UK!

Leicester City

The Grinders

The great Martin O'Neill arrived at Leicester City from Norwich City in December 1995. Within 16 months, he'd led the Foxes into the Premier League and had doubled their all-time trophy haul by beating Middlesbrough in the 1997 League Cup final replay, both games providing tactical masterclasses in suppressing the brilliant Juninho. O'Neill had transformed the City side with his futuristic brand of high-octane football – my, how the big boys sneered when defenders attacked and attackers tracked back! – and astute signings such as Muzzy Izzet from Chelsea, Steve Claridge from Blues and Neil Lennon from Crewe.

And the clueless press called them 'the grinders'; 'the world's greatest pub football team'. The Northern Ireland international was one of the finest holding midfielders City had ever seen, with an uncanny knack for reading the game. When O'Neill eventually moved on to Celtic, he broke Leicester hearts by returning to sign his gifted countryman.

The Coca-Cola Cup Final 1997 Replay

Leicester City v Middlesbrough

Liverpool

Weight in Silver

The way it's meant to work with enamel badges is that fans have the chance to buy a pin to commemorate the proudest day of their lives, when their lads won the League Cup or the ZDS Trophy at Wembley.

But if any Liverpool fan were foolish enough to wear a scarf hung with badges for all the silverware the Reds won in the '70s, '80s and '90s alone, they'd be walking with a permanent stoop.

Eleven League titles. Four FA Cups. Five League Cups. Four European and two UEFA Cups.

Not to mention made-up Super Cups and Charity jobs. It's called the weight of history.

Luton Town

In Glorious Technicolor

It may have been a smart look in the distant past but, by 1973, their plain old white shirts and black shorts were feeling decidedly drab in sunny Luton. A bit *monochromatic* in the

modern age of colour TV, psychedelic carpets and glam rock. So the Hatters decided to add a dash of colour to proceedings. Namely, a bright orange shirt with asymmetrical navy-and-white stripes, navy shorts and orange socks. The

jazzy, mind-blowing colourway worked wonders, and Luton were promptly promoted to the First Division.

Manchester City

Record Breaker

Eight long years have passed since we featured Eddie Sparrow's signed shirt in the City programme's 'Treasure Trove' slot. Back then it carried a cool 165 City star autographs; now it's up to 178. Surely, a record for any football shirt?

"The shirt is my pride and joy," Eddie said. "Every name on there is an original signing that I've collected up either by waiting outside the ground or training complex, or meeting the players somewhere else."

It's been a rollercoaster eight

years. While City have won four Premier League titles, Eddie has tragically lost both his father and his wife, Linda – prompting him to start a popular MCFC memorial Facebook page.

Manchester United

Fergie Time

Saturday 10th April 1993 marked the end of time as we knew it – when football matches

used to last 90 minutes – and into a new era of tactical flexibility. As United chased their first title in 26 years against Sheff Wednesday, stand-in ref John Hilditch appeared to allow Fergie's boys to play on for as

long as they needed to score, Steve Bruce finally netting a 96th-minute winner. From then on, Fergie took to strapping on

an assortment of United-friendly timepieces, standing tapping them on the touchline as a reminder of who was boss.

Middlesbrough

We Are the Champions

God knows, they took their time, keeping generations of fans waiting 128 years to break their duck with a solid chunk of major silverware.

They twice came perilously close in the 1996/97 season with a talented side that included the Brazilian pair, Juninho and Emerson, and the powerful Italian goalscorer Fabrizio Ravanelli, 'The White Feather'.

However, Boro lost out in the League Cup final to the 'Grinders' of Leicester, and then in the FA Cup final to Chelsea. The following season they lost again to Chelsea, this time in the League Cup. But in 2003/04, Boro finally lifted

a major trophy, beating both Tottenham Hotspur and Arsenal on the way to Wembley, where they successfully defeated Bolton Wanderers 2-1.

And then, would you believe, the engravers only went and spelled their name wrong on the bloody trophy!

Newcastle United

A Flying Buck

As popular as their great kits of the '60s-'90s may have been, not a lot of people know that the time-honoured Bukta logo was in fact a flying buck, named for the Manchester company, ER Buck & Sons, that originally produced football gear under the brand name as early as the 1880s.

The Magpies' Bukta shirt of 1978-80 was a cracker, this number 8 matchworn by Paul Cannell. The beautiful yellow away shirt is a number 7 worn by Stuart Barraclough, and the ultra-rare blue version also player-issued.

Nottingham Forest

Tricky Tree Trunks

When Brian Clough and Peter Taylor's Forest were First Division champions and then double European Cup winners, you couldn't blame any proud fan for wanting to log their

allegiance, whether in public or in private.

Back in the '80s, a pair of Forest swimming trunks could be more than enough to catch the eye of an admiring onlooker. Likwise, nylon club pants would always afford a warm glow

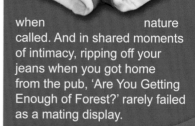

when   nature called. And in shared moments of intimacy, ripping off your jeans when you got home from the pub, 'Are You Getting Enough of Forest?' rarely failed as a mating display.

Norwich City

Stranger Than Fiction

Norwich City owe their 'Canaries' nickname to a group of 'Strangers' – 16th-century Dutch and Flemish refugees who brought their pets with them when they migrated to work as weavers.

As a result, canary breeding took off as a popular hobby across Norwich.

Contrary to myth, the club had no ties with the locally important Colman's Mustard of Carrow before the 1907 chairman, a keen canary fancier, changed the kit to yellow and green to match the team's nickname. It was just coincidence that mustard is also yellow – and that the club then moved to an enclosed ground on top of a hill... called 'The Nest'.

Two pints of Broon and a packet of crisps, please. Things about to get tasty between Walsh and Shearer.

Well preserved: The prospect of filling a folded card with jam jar lids had us scoffing for England.

fruit corner

The Football Dietician

Long before the time that 'five a day' sneakily became 'seven a day', the average footballer managed to get by quite happily on a fruit intake of approximately one half per week. All the vitamins, minerals and pips required used to be provided by the big, sour segments of orange we were given to suck on at half-time. Here's

Mick Mills and his trusty Ipswich boys drumming the wholesome message of 'half a week' into one of the development squad.

Of course, foodie fashion and awareness have changed greatly since the '70s and '80s, when we would supplement their diet with leaves and fruit from other sources numbering up to 40 a day. Fags, that is. And pots of jam.

Faced with the addictive prospect of filling a length of cardboard with jam jar lids featuring Ron Davies, the nation's kids embarked on an earnest jam-eating drive that saw fruit intake multiply fourfold and all HMG health targets surpassed. At the time it seemed to make more sense than joining Ray Clemence in a banana, even at a good retailer.

THEY'RE JUST IMPOSSIBLE TO SAVE.

Slot some Mini Jaffa Cakes into the corner of your lunchbox and you'll soon discover what makes them Man United's favourite half-time snack. Not only are they incredibly delicious, they're also low in fat and high in energy. No wonder they're so difficult to keep hold of. www.manutd.com/jeffacakes

Dynamic footballer Jimmy Greaves trains and scores on Bovril

RIGHT FROM THE START, Jimmy Greaves' football career has been an amazing success story.

He was one of the youngest players ever chosen for the England Under-23 International team, and he scored a goal within the first 10 minutes of his first appearance with the team in 1957.

As Chelsea's inside forward Jimmy has maintained his early promise, is now a full international player and one of the leading goal scorers in the Football League.

Jimmy, clearly marked for a great future in football, makes Bovril part of his training schedule. He says, "Like many other professional footballers, I take Bovril regularly all through the season. I thoroughly enjoy it – wouldn't be without it in fact. Bovril is a big help when it comes to keeping you at the top of your form."

BOVRIL does you a power of good

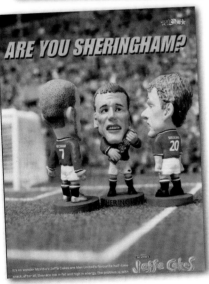

ARE YOU SHERINGHAM?

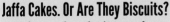

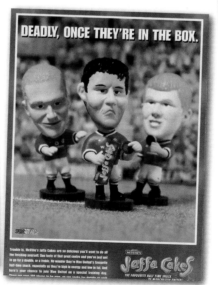

DEADLY, ONCE THEY'RE IN THE BOX.

BOVRIL ONE OF THE PLEASURES OF LEISURE

Jaffa Cakes. Or Are They Biscuits?

Fast forward to the '90s and another ad campaign that gave fruit consumption a healthy boost.

Corinthian figures were then a huge cult, so bringing the little moulded figures 'to life' was marketing genius combined with a battery of quality footballing puns. Every aspect of the campaign was a triumph. Except for every Corinthian collector's greatest joy – a weirdly unrecognisable figure. The 'David Beckham' that you'd have bet your house was meant to be Wes Brown...

Bovril Boys

Just as attitudes have changed to obesity and vitamin deficiency, so dead animals have suffered a recent downturn in public perception. Although it's still a classic half-time winter warmer for fans, Bovril doesn't now have the feel of a health drink. Where dynamic young Jimmy Greaves used to 'take' Bovril to help him score, we can't quite picture a modern star talking up training on a cuppa dissolved meat. Cheers!

Gordon Banks' top breakfast was Shredded Wheat with fried eggs. Mmmmmm!

CUP SOCCER 71
NEWCASTLE UNITED 8

CUP SOCCER 71
DERBY COUNTY 3

CUP SOCCER 71
CHELSEA 2

CUP SOCCER 71
MANCHESTER UNITED 7

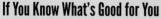

If You Know What's Good for You

Good old Nabisco used to serve up a splendid range of football collectables with our breakfast cereal on schooldays, a new box of Shredded Wheat prompting an exciting hunt through the box that more than made up for the fact that the cereals themselves tasted like small, fossilised mattresses. Jackie Charlton and Brian Clough appeared in '90s TV ads where it was bizarrely suggested that Gary Lineker (or anyone in their right mind) might have been willing or

able to eat three of the things.

It wasn't just Cup Soccer pamphlets, football cards, club badges and Bob Wilson's Soccer Action stickers that came free with Shreded Wheat; you could get free World Cup final seats as well. The trick was to search for the bulky-looking packets in Fine Fare.

As the next least attractive breakfast cereal, it was only fitting that Weetabix should also call in heavyweight influencers to try and convince us to ask for them. Almost incredibly, they enlisted

the help of The Weetabix – a reggae band made up of Cockney skinhead football yobboes who happened to have been born wheat biscuits. Actor Bob Hoskins did his East End gangster voice for

108

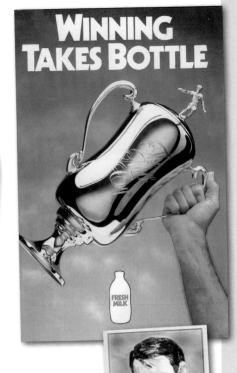

Michael Owen of England, long past the Mike and Mick era.

milky milky

MILK

FOR NOURISHMENT AND ENERGY
NORTH STAFFS CO-OPERATIVE
DAIRY Tel: 24616

the lead Weetabix, threatening us to eat up 'if you know what's good for you'.

Today only sugar and Mike Ashley that can boast an approval rating lower than bullyish cereal-based ska acts, hence Sugar Puffs are now known as Honey Monster Puffs. The lovable monster, his Supreme Team and pencil-topper shirt collection were among the very highest points of '90s culture.

The White Stuff

Like Bovril, jam and Jaffa Cakes, milk's once-powerful association with top-class sport has suffered a 21st-century decline.

Yes, yes, yes, we all know it's full of calcium and potassium and vitamin D and enough latent oomph to turn a cute baby calf into a fearsome bull. But there's no hardcore marketing push behind moo-moo any more. Milk isn't

fizzy, and doesn't cost an arm and a leg for a designer titanium canister of the stuff. Footballers don't get paid to put it on their cornflakes or bathe in it, Cleopatra style, so kids think it's boring.

Coh, we remember when players would swig down whole bottles of the stuff after the FA Cup final – hmm, or maybe that was the *Milk* Cup final?

Either way, let's bring it back!

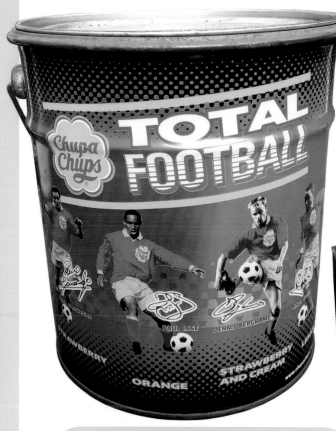

Surrealism and Soccer

Quiz question for you: What is Salvador Dali's link with Sheffield Wednesday Football Club?

Our first guess was something to do with the club's stylised owl badge which dates back to 1973, so could potentially have been the work of the Spanish surrealist. But surely we'd already know if that were the case?

Give up? The answer lies with the Owls' shirt sponsor at the turn of the millennium – the Spanish lollipop company, Chupa Chups.

Although the logo on the lolly wrappers (and our giant Total Football counter tin) features not a single melting clock, it was designed by Dali himself in 1969.

Some Candy Talking

Catering to a more youthful market than their toxic fore-runners, sweet cigarettes always had one important thing in common with the traditional tobacco variety. Every pack came with a collector card.

Even when political correctness demanded they be renamed 'candy sticks' – as if removing the dab of red on the end would ever stop kids pretending to light up – the cards retained classic 'ciggie card' dimensions, an unwholesome throwback to flogging a bad habit to unsuspecting Victorians.

Barratt's started producing confectionery cards back in the 1920s, and even when they were taken over by Bassett's in 1966, their trainer fags and junior cig cards retained the brand name up until the end of the '90s.

They always seemed a bit too small to us, offering too few cards for your shiny new 2p piece. But, hey. One man's candy is another man's poison, eh?

Start collecting All Stars!

Introducing All Stars! Great new crunchy snacks from Golden Wonder in two smashing flavours – Crispy Bacon and Salt 'n' Vinegar. But what's really great is that you get a free picture-card of one of Britain's top soccer stars in every pack – absolutely free! And there's a tremendous album to send in for!

So start your All Stars collection now! There are 24 soccer stars in the set.

New Crunchy Golden Wonder ALL STARS

THERE'S A FREE PICTURE-CARD IN EVERY PACK

Welcome to Crisp City

As a native of Leicester, there's no doubt which aspect of the city's rich history gives us the second greatest sense of local pride.

Richard III, Showaddywaddy and Sue Townsend come close, but add up the sheer pleasure provided over the decades and our status as crisp capital of Britain brings a tear to the eye. In Leicester, bar snacks are in our blood.

As a school leaver, the mood of the day was determined by the flavour in the air, wafting citywide from the Walker's factory. The big friendly crisp giant sponsored Leicester City from 1987 to 2001, giving us our very own 'Roy of the Rovers'-style comic strip – and then a name for our new stadium.

Watching the old crisp ads on YouTube, Gary Lineker's 'Welcome Home' is a 1995 Coritanian classic, bettered only by the one where he crunches Gazza's hand in his bag and makes him cry.

As if all this weren't enough, there's Golden Wonder, too. Must-have All-Star cards, Wotsit stickers and priceless Whooshers, the finest ever foodie football freebies.

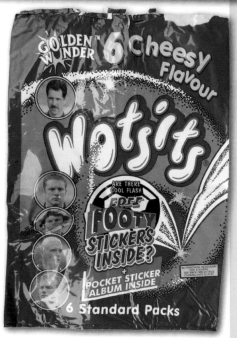

FREE from Ty·Phoo TEA

Colour print of your favourite football team— and club rosette

WHEN YOU COLLECT 24 FOOTBALL CARDS FROM TY·PHOO TEA PACKETS

A big colour print of your favourite football team, measuring 10 inches by 8 inches, and a bright taffeta rosette in the club colours for you to wear! They're free for you from Ty·Phoo.

Just collect 24 different "Famous Football Club" cards — there's one on the side of every Ty·Phoo packet, telling you the history of a famous League club. Send these in to Ty·Phoo and tell us the name of your favourite team amongst the twenty-four leading clubs in the series. Ty·Phoo will send you an up-to-date colour print and rosette.

Start collecting Ty·Phoo packets now and you'll have those 24 cards in no time.

Is Arsenal your favourite team ? It's just one of the 24 you can choose from.

Send your complete set of 24 cards to:— TY·PHOO TEA LIMITED, DEPT. F, Birmingham 5.

KEITH NEWTON (Blackburn Rovers and England)

A NEW SERIES OF FOOTBALL STARS

Ty·Phoo TEA

The T that stands for Taste

4oz NET

BURNLEY F.C.

DEREK DOUGAN (Wolverhampton Wanderers and Northern Ireland)

fancy a brew?

SUNDERLAND F.C.

RODNEY MARSH (Queens Park Rangers and England 'Under 23')

A NEW SERIES OF FOOTBALL STARS

Ty·Phoo TEA

No. 18 Bobby Moore

Ty-Phoo Put the T in Football

For years they were considered highly collectable, the handsome 10" by 8" cardboard player photos that fans used to send off for from Ty-Phoo Tea. Popular stars regularly fetched around a tenner apiece. Although the earlier teamgroups from 1963 and '65 still command these prices, the huge, open online market has exposed just how common the player sets were back in the day. Today there are 19 Georgie Bests on eBay (charting hair growth from 1967 to '69 and '73), and four have sold recently for under £2 each.

Ironically, the black-and-white cards on the tea packet side panels, once exchangeable at a rate of 12 for one, are worth that much.

But the real premium find is the complete original packets, understandably now in very short supply. Happy days if you've got any complete with the tea inside!

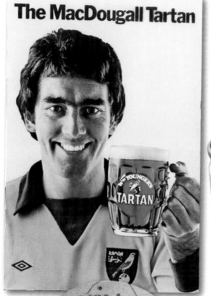

The MacDougall Tartan

BUY A BASS EXPORT AND SEE THE 1970 WORLD CUP IN MEXICO

10 Luxury holidays for two in Mexico for the 1970 World Cup

PLUS 1,000 runner–up prizes

GET YOUR ENTRY FORM AT THE BAR

DROP IN FOR A DRINK

VAUX

Blackpool F.C.

The winning combination.

VAUX BREWERIES · OFFICIAL TEAM SPONSORS.

ACTUALLY, I BET HE DRINKS CARLING BLACK LABEL

Here's to the Thirst Division

From the Benskins Pennant Supporters Club

Only Here for the Beer

We're all used to seeing beer ads on players' shirts, but it now seems a while since stars were pictured downing pints. And even longer since clubs such as Man United, Arsenal, Everton and Liverpool endorsed their own branded lager, which was extremely short lived.

Our old friend Ryan Herman unearthed the story for vice.com – how Essex entrepreneur Kenny Willmott did a lucrative deal with the clubs and Cornish Breweries.

In December 1987, Man United held an OT launch party for Red Devil lager, and the *Daily Mail* hit moral outrage mode. 'CANNED FOR THE FANS – storm as top clubs label their own lager'. The paper proclaimed that the clubs were 'accused of encouraging hooliganism'. United's additional marketing idea didn't help matters. By collecting Red Devil ring pulls, fans could claim free gifts. Collect 640 and you could get into Old Trafford for free instead of paying

the £3.20 it then cost to stand on the Stretford End!

Within 24 hours of its official launch, Manchester United Red Devil was effectively canned, soon followed by Everton Premium Lager and Liverpool Super Reds.

Notts County

Nice One Sirrel

Out of all the statuary ever placed outside football grounds, from Billy Bremner to Michael Jackson, we'd nominate Notts County's Jimmy Sirrel tribute as our favourite.

The likeness of the Magpies' long-time manager is uncanny and, sitting on his bench on Meadow Lane with assistant Jack Wheeler, you wouldn't be too surprised if the larger-than-life statue started talking old-school tactics in a

deep Glasgow accent.

Jimmy is spookily impressive. It can't be easy to make those woolly sheepskin collars or credible string-backed driving gloves out of cast bronze.

QPR

Rod-ney, Rod-ney Rattle

Two generations of fans now exist that have never seen (or

heard) a rattle at a football match. Many younger fans would presumably even struggle

Portsmouth

Play Up Pompey

Thanks go out to Sean Simpson of Portsmouth who answered our plea for Pompey memorabilia with this item from the PFC museum in his loft – open to selected guests, by invitation only!

This little figurine's classic kit reflects the fleeting trend in the early '70s when so many clubs decided to give up their traditional colours for a trendy white version. Leicester City, Hearts, Bradford City and others were all at it, along with Pompey.

Also interestingly, Sean reports that the figure was a tie-in with Brooke-Bond's 'Play Better Soccer' series of tea cards. We always think a complete album of those great little cards, however common, should be worth more than a quid to any collector.

to recognise one of these fated victims of Health & Safety, let alone know what it was for.

Well, just for the record, rattles make a deafening clacking racket and have the ability to give your neighbour a joyful whack on the ear when a goal goes in. They first appeared on the terraces after World War I when Tommies brought home their gas-attack warning rattles from the trenches.

Here's a beauty, customised in traditional style in QPR colours, complete with tribute to Loftus Road hero, Rodney Marsh.

Rangers

Oor Willie

You might think that the sight of a sea of inflatables at a football match only became commonplace after August 1987, when the banana craze first took hold among Manchester City fans. In fact, the first ever football

inflatables date back as far as mid-'60s Glasgow.

While Celtic fans waved custom-made 'Jinky' figures, apparently modelled on winger Jimmy Johnstone, our Rangers spokesman believes this strikingly similar blue-and-white blow-up was produced around the same time.

"Our inflatables were called 'Willies'," he commented. "They were based on our winger, Willie Henderson."

Sheffield United

Blades Are Back

With Sheffield United back in the top tier, it seems fitting to recall these rare stickers from the FKS 'demo' album of 1967/68. Sadly, by the time the album was made commercially available nationwide the following season, the Blades were down – and out.

Aside from a single season's Match Attax cards and Merlin stickers in 2006/07, the last time the Blades featured in a major series was in 1993/94 Merlin, a year after the Prem's inaugural season, which saw Brian Deane score the League's first goal in a 2-1 win against Manchester United.

SHEFFIELD UNITED F. C.

Sheffield Wednesday

Friends in High Places

Back in May 1982, I visited a mate at Sheffield University who was a Chelsea fan. The trip coincided with the Sheff Wed-Chelsea game, and gave me the rare chance to experience one of the greatest views in British football history – from the vast, uncovered Hillsborough Kop.

Standing near the extended back of this man-made mountain

OFFICIAL PROGRAMME — SIXPENCE

FOOTBALL LEAGUE DIVISION ONE

SHEFFIELD WEDNESDAY
versus
BLACKBURN ROVERS

EASTER MONDAY, 15th APRIL, 1963.
KICK-OFF 3.0 P.M.

Football at Hillsborough

LAST MATCH ON THE UNCOVERED
KOP!
3·5·86
S.W.F.C v
IPSWICH

gave us a fantastic

eagle's-eye view of the pitch as well as beyond the ground, out of the city and up the looming moors' rocky bluffs, bathed in sunshine.

Even today, now it's covered and seated, an ancient oblique gangway still traces the slope of the old 1914 Kop up to the top corner.

Southampton

Get Yer Echo

It takes a special kind of collector to be forever alert to potential gems. While lesser devotees merely celebrated

Saints winning the '76 Cup final, Martin Bennett was busy pilfering (sorry, *acquiring*) unique future memorabilia from the city's newsstands. We don't half wish we'd thought of that.

Stoke City

Sort of Stripes

Being a kit designer is all about giving the fans what they want. Or, at least, what they *would*

want, if they weren't so hung up on stupid old traditions. Kit designers have to be granted creative freedom, right? Otherwise Stoke's kit would always just be red-and-white stripes, like Umbro had been producing with minimal variations since the early '70s – following on from a history of similar red-and-white stripes cascading all the way back to before the First World War. So, in 1983, a new visionary at Umbro gave them

something different. It was *sort of* stripy. And two years later they were back in proper stripes. Forever.

Sunderland

The Roker Pager

"Keeps you up to date with all the exciting team, club, player and match news as it happens - direct from *your* club!"

That was the basic proposition used to convince Sunderland fans to get a club pager. Not convinced? Oh, you will be...

"With the personal pager facility on your Roker Pager you can also set the trends. Paging is no longer the domain of companies and organisations. Millions of private individuals across the world use pagers in their personal, social and family lives to improve the quality of their life."

Ready to do the deal yet?

"Relax in the knowledge that you can be contacted. Give

the pager to other members of your family when they go out... YOUR DINNER IS IN THE DOG... TIME TO COME HOME... TURN AROUND AND COME BACK, I CAN'T MEET YOU!"

And so to the final, desperate pleas for your cash...

"Less intrusive than a cellular phone, and much much cheaper.

"Make the most of your life. Live it to the full – with the Roker Pager!"

Houston, we have a problem: Man United's Stewart and family lose the front door key.

WATFORD F.C.

ASTON VILLA PREPARED

LEEDS UNITED A.F.C

SHREWSBURY TOWN FC 1886 CENTENARY YEAR 1986

NEWCASTLE UNITED F.C F.A. CUP FINALISTS 1974

Trendy Crockery Dept.

As a fan of wealth and taste, you're bound to be aware how *on trend* our kitchen selection is, here at Gift Book Towers. Like all the finest bijou restaurants in North London, we've slaked off the old-fashioned stigma around being poor and disorganised, and have learned to revel in our mixed, upcycled furniture and mismatched crockery. Welcome to our dinner party!

1 – In 1973, Alan Sunderland was still with Wolves. He's let us use this picture from four years before he joined the Highbury elite, to warn *how not to do it* in the kitchen. We can now smile affectionately at Alan's catalogue dinner service, his cardigan and signature 'A'-shaped hairdo; though, ironically, his flowery curtains are back with a bang, and the greasy extractor fan is making waves among those in the know.

2 – Great news for Cov fans, who haven't had much to cheer about of late. Now you can eat locally sourced delicacies off the faces of Sky Blue heroes like Ernie Hunt.

WORLD SPAIN '82 CUP BULLDOG BOBBY

what's cooking?

DID YOU KNOW ONLY FAMOUS MUGS GET ON SMUGS®?

WELL THAT'S ALWAYS BEEN MY GOAL!

Smugs® - the unique 3 dimensional life-like mug, officially authorised and bearing the signature of the player. Everyone will want to collect their footballing favourites. Smugs® are really tough in the field. Unlike the real

thing they don't 'crack' under pressure or cry if they get 'dropped'. So get down to your local store and start collecting now! Look out for new sporting additions to the Smugs® range appearing soon.

SOCCER Stars

3 – Seriously vintage crockery. Who knew Watford played in blue, before the days of Elton and their lurid umber, ruby and jet combo?
4 – An infant Nigel Pearson lurks on a Shrews plate with an stylised logo only now gaining recognition among fans as a design classic.
5 – Ditto the three-legged fox.
6 – Stylish CFC frying fan, perfect for those occasions when only pan-fried or pan-seared will do.

7 – Alas, it's time for our guests to 'do the honours' and help with the washing-up. How lucky that the silverware summaries on our vintage Ipswich and Saints tea-towels have both aged really well!

Smug

We hear of shock images reaching these shores from South-East Asia via the new-fangled internet. Fine diners tucking into monkeys'

brains without first paying the unsuspecting beasts the courtesy of a quick, dignified end.

To be frank, it's rather put us off the USP of these vintage Smug collectables, which offered fans the singular pleasure of drinking a cuppa direct from the bonce of a selection of stars. Who wants their coffee tainted by essence of Gullit or Seaman? Give us our brew in a Bill Shankly Toby jug, any day.

In the Boodwah

We all know that bedtime can be quite exciting, but the prospect of snuggling down under a football bedspread is almost enough to keep you awake all night. Especially if you're doing your bonus star-studded jigsaw by torchlight under the covers.

This sensational Leeds United continental quilt comes closest of all to embodying the 1970s in a single item. It's the combination of the 'Smiley' badge with other designs from Coffer Sports' range of sew-on patches that does the trick. Ahh, that superb 'V for Victory' sign that was only ever seen in 'American comics', on denim jackets or a hippie's jean pocket. That supercool 'Nice One' reference. Plus the almost casual namedrop of 'bionic' Leeds thrown in for good measure, conjuring images of Steve Austin

running in slow-motion across the Elland Road pitch. And his girlfriend Jaime Sommers hearing him coming with her bionic ear.

Star Wars

Following the lead of star players, who eventually complained about their unlicensed appearance on sundry laundry and household

time for bed

If you really have to be woken up for school, it may as well be by Frank Worthington.

goods, many of the bigger clubs became more marketing aware during the '80s and '90s. If anyone was going to make 100% polyester 'jamas with scant regard for real kit styles or club badges, it was blooming well going to be Spurs and Arsenal themselves.

The marketing man's dream bedroom was draped in official wallpaper, branded soft furnishings and electrical goods, and bore little resemblance to reality. A home-made shrine evolved in most kids' rooms, where admission was strictly guarded by a pottery team plaque, and birthday presents from well-meaning aunties were clustered on shelves beneath the gaze of star portraits from *Shoot!* and *Match* looming from every wall. Lamps, piggy banks and novelty ornaments were affectionate local tributes or generic 'football fan' gifts, as hit-or-miss as the 'You Are 12' soccer birthday card. Like young Paul Owens in his Neville Southall shinpads, we learned to put up with the odd rogue red clock in an otherwise determined DIY colour scheme.

CHELSEA FOOTBALL CLUB

BLUES • BLUES

STAMFORD BRIDGE

Steve Heighway plays it clean.

Steve Heighway. Liverpool and Republic of Ireland, B.Sc (Econ.) is a superstar at 22. He plays it clean — on and off the field. Steve knows the value of keeping in good physical shape. He relies on training, a balanced diet and pHisoHex.

pHisoHex is an antibacterial skin cleanser that surgeons all over the world rely on for germ-free hands both before and after operations. And doctors prescribe it for spots and acne.

He knows that regular washing with pHisoHex together with thorough rinsing, will clean out the dirt, grease and germs that encourage spots.

Play it clean on and off the field with pHisoHex.

Like Steve Heighway.

For a free copy of the Teenage Acne Booklet please write to: Mrs G. Usher, Winthrop Laboratories, Dept. G2, Winthrop House, Surbiton-upon-Thames, Surrey.

pHisoHex at your chemist's. For skin as clean as a surgeon's hands.

October 2 1971   GOAL   25

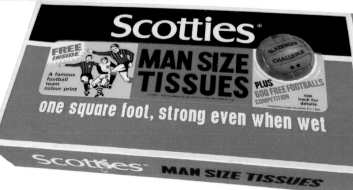

PETER SOLVES HIS PROBLEM and the GIRLS COME RUNNING

GOAL!

TACKLE MEDICATED CLEAR GEL FOR MEN

Scotties MAN SIZE TISSUES
FREE INSIDE — A famous football team colour print
PLUS 600 FREE FOOTBALLS COMPETITION see back for details
SLAZENGER CHALLENGE
one square foot, strong even when wet
Scotties MAN SIZE TISSUES

Bathroom Dept.

Ground floor perfumery, stationery and leather goods... Going up!

Which is to say we're still stuck here by the revolving doors near the entrance of the grand Gift Book department store. The air is a heady fug of scents and solvents, shampoos and medications, just like when your mum used to drag you round the perfume counters in Boots, using your wrists as testers because she'd only got two of her own and she didn't want them to get mixed up. The scents, that is.

So... could we perhaps interest you in a bottle of Steve Heighway's skin cleanser? Otherwise you'll smell faintly for days of Phil Parkes' Cossack, Kevin Keegan's Brut 33 and Georgie Best's Fore.

Be smart, like Steve. Play it clean on and off the field. pHisoHex might not have the catchiest name but it beats bacteria. The key question is: will it help you score?

Are you going to trust an economics graduate's knowledge of chemistry, or fall for a nudge-wink football pun and an even weaker promise of sexual activity?

Aw, heck. Let's go for a big tub of Tackle and the 5,000-to-1 shot that we really are mates with the Captain in his flash sports car, that there really is a '2nd Girl' with a keen eye for 'wasted talent'.

While we're doing beauty, best grab some FA Carling Premiership (1993-2001) razors to help make the right first impression in your CFC shaving mirror. And a man-size box of tissues with another outside chance – of a free football. Plus a 'famous football team print' of real rarity value, that must be worth a bob or two today.

Forever Filbo

Here's lifelong Leicester City fan, Mike Gurr, sitting for the last time in the Supporters' Club corner at Filbert Street. The old ground was sadly demolished back in 2002 but Mike had a canny plan to rescue some relics for old times' sake.

Even today, Mike can enjoy sitting outside in chilly discomfort, moaning happily with up to three mates about relegation, pie prices and that bloody Peter Taylor.

Fun on the Lawn Lawn Lawn

Just when you thought there wouldn't be much in the *Gift Book* Garden section, it turns out there are more lawn and rockery ornaments based on former Leeds chairman Ken Bates than you'd ever have credited. You can even get cool commemorative statues, like this proud Billy McNeill, leader of your lawn's Lisbon Lions.

Garden Goals

Do you remember when it *really was* like Wembley in your garden? When dad's twin ornamental cherries magically transformed

the great outdoors

into a yawning net, with only Simon Ball to beat to win the Cup?

Or maybe you were a bit spoilt, and got an an *actual* garden goal to play in with your posh so-called mates. No, no, we're not jealous. Not much. But, like Howard Tomlinson (Man Utd) and his brother Anthony (Spurs, controversially), our privations

did teach us to tap into the power of our imaginations. Here's H and A on big-match day, before it all kicked off at Old Trafford.

garden gates

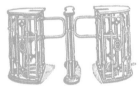

In for Free

There are big benefits to owning your own turnstile from a long-defunct stadium. The memories come flooding back at every clunk. The very act of preservation is important, for future generations. Not forgetting, of course, you can now get in for free.

1 – "I bought the main turnstile to Pen 3 of the Kop at the Filbert Street auction," says City fan Chris Hinsley. " It took four of us to move it as all the concrete was still attached! No garden is complete without a 1927 turnstile."

2 – Our old mate Andy McConachie has a rare Ellison's model from the Baseball Ground in his Derby garden.

3 – "Here's my turnstile from the old Boleyn Ground," says Neil McNair, rightfully proud of his installation at the Old Mill Guest House in the Yorkshire Dales. "It was from the old East Stand, purchased at auction prior to demolition. I was a season-ticket holder for 25 years before moving up north, so it's a constant reminder of all those Saturdays spent watching the Hammers play at this great stadium."

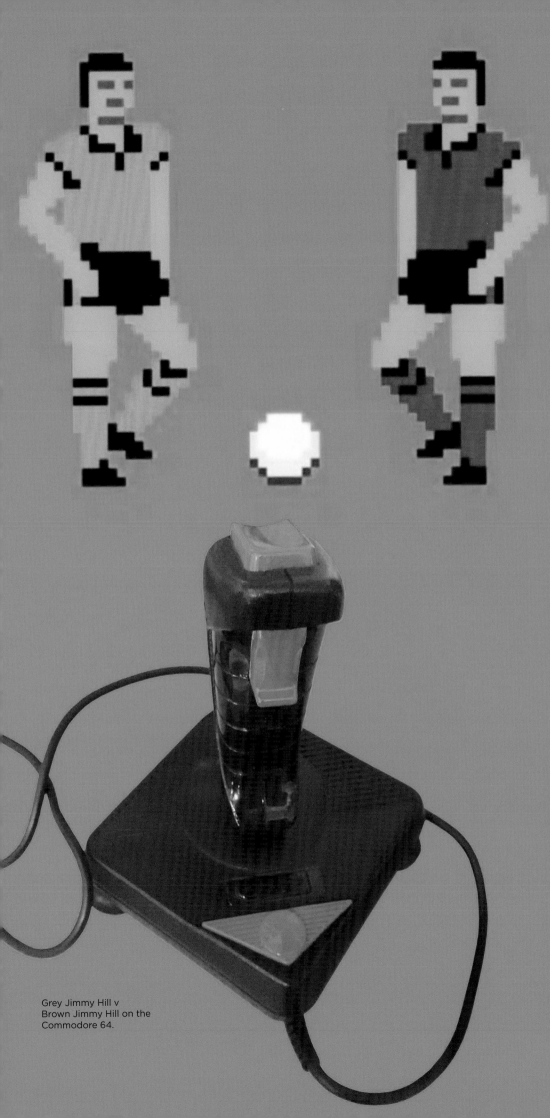

Grey Jimmy Hill v
Brown Jimmy Hill on the
Commodore 64.

3-D!

Enjoy the View-Master

The vintage View-Master handed down by my cousin, Kay, is one of my favourite things. Delve into her big box of slides, slip one into the slot and I'm instantly on a 3-D Technicolor holiday in London or on the Continent in the '60s, diving in coral reefs or right there among the stars of a Disney film.

Spotting a bargain set of three 1962 World Cup slides on eBay for two quid, I couldn't wait to take my place out on the virtual pitch. So imagine my surprise when the slides arrived and the content wasn't quite as billed. Yes, I could opt out of reality and into a fantasy world of soccer, only it wasn't at the World Cup. Instead, I was sent swirling down a 3-D Time Tunnel to a series of Dutch second division matches in the '70s.

Now the detective work starts, to find out exactly when and where I'm wandering. And to find out how much this accidental treasure is worth on the Dutch market!

Tech Treasures from Lost Time

Just imagine the envious looks you'll get at the big match when you put on your pair of powerful Tele-Specs – and suddenly it's like you're out there in the goalmouth alongside your heroes and the luminous oppo goalie.

Many of the keenest fans are now using their telescopic glasses along with a patent Superfan loud hailer, which gives you the power to direct words of encouragement direct into your team's ears.

And when you're back at school on Monday, look up next weekend's fixtures on a superbly engraved ruler in first-grade anti-static plastic. Yours for two bob.

Full-backs Robson and Webster: 'Derby's Supertwins'.
Not to be confused with a washing machine.

THEY DON'T HAVE TO STOP AT HALF TIME.

CANON LEAGUE DIVISION O
Saturday, 24th August, 1985. Kick-off 3.00 p.m.

Ipswich town

50p   v.   TOTTENHAM HOTSPUR

Radio Orwell

257 Radio Orwell OFFICIAL CLUB SPONSORS

240   **Saxon Radio**   240

Batteries Not Included

Here's the stars of Derby County admiring the hot gadgets at C&A Electrics in town – 'the best team in the domestic appliance division'. Watney Cup winners Terry Hennessey, John Robson and Roy McFarland are thrilled to see a Hoover advertised by Dave Mackay ('the best sweeper in the business') and a tumble drier with Willie Carlin's stamp of approval ('small, but what a performer!').

The lads from Man United are enjoying ultra-modern hi-fi gear. 'Thanks to Sharp, they don't have to change round at half-time when they're playing their favourite records. The astonishing VZ music machines have a vertical turntable that actually plays both sides of a record, without turning it over. VZ is the latest word in disc technology, making records every bit as easy to play as cassettes.'

Meanwhile, Ipswich keeper Paul Cooper shows how you can listen to music on the go with a Philips cassette player and radio that Paul always keeps tuned to 257 for Radio Orwell. The unit is fully shoulder portable, only weighing as much as a small bag of cement.

And you'll never be late for kick-off again with a Liquid Crystal Display ('LCD') watch individually designed with your name and the badge of your favourite football team. The must-have item of 1979.

Missing in Action:
Nowadays, they won't
even take videotapes at
charity shops. The bloody
ingrates.

VHS Rules OK

If you've got a touch of the
nostalgic about you, it's hard to
admit that anything in the present
day trumps its more innocent and
understandable equivalent from
your formative years.

No one today thinks of BBC
i-Player, On Demand, Netflix, 749
cable channels or downloading a
box set for free as a welcome leap
in entertainment accessability.
They're just here, unbidden, and
we take them for granted.

What we yearn for instead
is those days when there were
only three or four channels, and
everyone was forced to watch *The
Generation Game* at exactly the
same time on Saturday evening,
otherwise we'd miss it.

Or maybe the small screen's true
Golden Era was the mind- and
time-expanding dawn of the VHS
and the VCR, when we enjoyed
our precious first taste of having a
choice in when we watched what
we watched. Tapping into this dark

magick, it even became possible to
videotape a TV programme *while
you were watching something else
on the other side.*

It felt we were somehow cheating
natural law when we stumbled in
late and still got to watch *Match
of the Day.* The VCR provided a
Time Tunnel direct to your team's
greatest games, golden goals and
godawful gaffs, Danny Baker style.

And, for a few short years, we
truly appreciated the new-found
ability to bend time to our will.

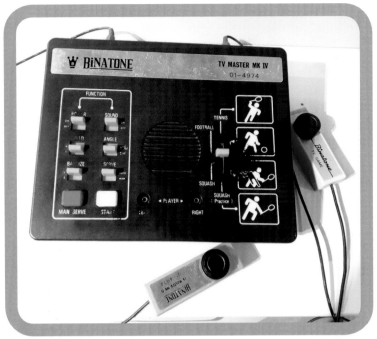

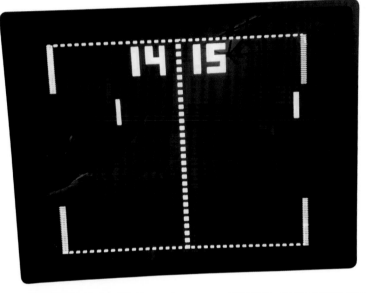

Binatone Beep Boop

If the chance to watch your very own personal VCR rerun of *Kojak* changed your world, then the ability to take physical control of events on a television screen was enough to shift the entire planet on its axis.

For the first time, it was possible to hook up a state-of-art electronic box to your bossy old telly and tell it what to do for a change.

Originally released by Atari in 1972, Pong was one of the most revolutionary, addictive arcade games ever seen. It wasn't until 1977 that home TV and handheld versions of the game began to appear, from manufacturers such as Binatone, Grandstand and Prinztronic. While the detail in the soccer game wasn't quite up to the lifelike version of tennis (they were pretty much the same game), it was still a unique, once-in-a-lifetime thrill to twist a knob or jerk a joystick and feel the power over a virtual game that would shortly change life and society beyond recognition.

Beep... boop... beep... and now you're hopelessly obsessed.

Do you remember the pride you felt when you first learned to 'spin' a ball with a stylish flick of the wrist? Is it, in fact, possible to 'spin' a ball on any Pong platform? Did you used to play on the tricky 'acute angle' setting? Er, anyone for a game of Tank Battle?

You're the Boss

Wheeeeeekkk! It was an odd, high-pitched shriek that accompanied a video game cassette tape loading on to your home computer, and so on to your TV screen. The most exciting noise imaginable.

In 1982, Kevin Toms launched the original Football Manager simulation game, available for Dragon 32 and Amstrads but soon ported to Amiga, Atari, BBC, Commodore and PC systems. Written in BASIC code, the game was text-only with stick-man highlights on some systems. Still powerful enough to see your side promoted from division four to one. And to make you suspect you may be the new Cloughie.

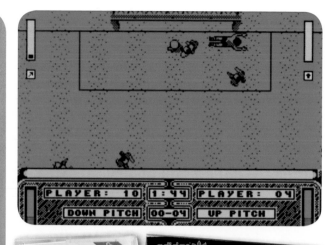

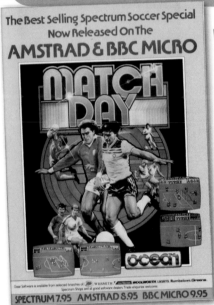

The Best Selling Spectrum Soccer Special
Now Released On The
AMSTRAD & BBC MICRO

MATCH DAY

ocean

SPECTRUM 7.95 AMSTRAD 8.95 BBC MICRO 9.95

beyond console

adidas
CHAMPIONSHIP FOOTBALL

TAKE ON THE WORLD!
automatic team response
the choice of all football players,
YOU MAKE THE PLAY!

ATARI ST CBM AMIGA
ocean

Sinclair ZX Spectrum

In-between 1979's genesis of football gaming with Mattel's NASL Soccer (on the Intellivision console) and today's market bossed by the current evolutionary leaders, countless platforms and games have come and gone. Some good, some bad. In any case, hundreds too many to mention. So here's a short catalogue selection of hits and misses on every scale.

While Football Manager kicked off the football management simulation model, Match Day was also popular on the ZX Spectrum, closely based on the live-action model of NASL Soccer. Even at this early stage, you got to control one player at a time, and could choose to play against an opponent or the computer itself. Yes, it was stick-man basic, but the automatic handling of corners and

throws was neat, players did have little coded quirks of personality – and the ability to control the goalie would be appreciated by any infant FIFA addict.

Commodore 64

Breaking with the popular 'camera view' of NASL Soccer (marketed as International Soccer for the C64), 4 Soccer Simulators scrolled vertically up and down a red pitch,

offering extra options in Soccer Skills, Indoor and Street Soccer. None were very convincing. By the turn of the '90s more was expected from gameplay than the mini World Cup served up in overhead view in Championship Football. Apart from the confusing name, the start-up selecting groups was overlong and stoopidly built in no seeding; there was no two-player mode, and it actually wasn't possible to control your men with one joystick and just two hands.

Sega Mega Drive

The box for Super Kick Off claims it's 'Europe's No.1 soccer game', and it's true that many of the

contemporay press reviews found online give it high scores across the board, criticising only its high price of £45. Like its predecessor Kick Off games (for the Amiga and Atari ST) it used a vertical view, kicking up and down the screen. It even made the jump to the Super Nintendo and Game Boy. Maybe you had to be there.

Atari ST

First released for the Amiga and Atari in 1992, Sensible Soccer is recognised as the landmark football game that paved the way forward. It retains a cult following of fans who prefer it to its modern successors and, even without the

nostalgia factor, could still be enjoyed by a modern gamer brat.

Building on the piecemeal offering of earlier games, it featured teams from every professional league on the planet. Gameplay wasn't realistic by today's standards but the bird's-eye view of the pitch remains iconic.

Most importantly, Sensi enabled you to transfer players between clubs, foreshadowing the USP of not only FIFA and PES but also Football Manager.

Looking back, it signalled the parting of the ways for the two game types. The sense of control over your team was all new, as you could choose your tactics and set about picking up players who would fit into your system.

Anatomy of the modern footballer

- Improved intelligence. Players move off the ball, provide better service and more accurate passes.

- New volleys – and you'll need it to go one-on-one with these smarter 'keepers.
- Goals come from volleys, half-volleys and swerving banana shots.

- Over 200 international teams.
- Play a complete domestic league season, then take your team on tour abroad.

- Pick up a niggling injury and you could be out for the season.

- Bullet headers on goal, beyond the reach of the diving 'keeper.

- Harder shots!
- Faster players!
- Stronger passes!

- Score from deadly set play free kicks.

FIFA 98 v 2020: Bring back the cheaty dive and the dirty tackle button!

And the Winners?

One day, gamers are bound to look back at these pages and smirk at the idea that Football Manager should be the current leader of the race toward 100% realism in the management simulation stakes. It's been a turbulent story so far, with FM successfully carrying forward the legacy of Championship Manager after ownership of the popular '90s series was split in 2003, setting CM against FM.

Likewise, the series kicked off by FIFA International Soccer in 1993 was quick to migrate across platforms with FIFA 95 and 96, and is now licensed to the hilt, top dog in football match simulation. But there are signs of a PES (Pro Evolution Soccer) resurgence...

Nothing lasts forever in football's doppelgänger world, the only certainty that the virtual game will continue to appear ever more real.

Now that players are spending real money in-game on pixels – aka enhanced player packs for FIFA – the alarming sci-fi vision of Philip K Dick is finally upon us. What price a Perky Pat layout and a dose of Can-D to maximise the benefit of your latest acquisitions?

Sony scores again

Someone's got to be champion and when it comes to colour TV our new 13" Trinitron colour set takes some beating.
Built with Sony's world famous solid-state circuitry it's fully transistorised and so reliable that we can give you a 2 year guarantee on the tube and a 5 year guarantee on all transistors.
The picture?—What a picture! You'll have no doubts about who scored which off what when you see the big match on this little masterpiece.

The secret's in our single gun tube which incorporates a huge electron lens that gives a sharper, clearer picture than conventional TV. And because it's transistorised the Trinitron KV 1320 UB weighs just 39lb which means it can be easily carried for room to room viewing. Spectacular for sport—marvellous for movies —a delight for documentaries. Sony Trinitron, a winner all the way.
Sony Trinitron recommended retail price £192·30

The choice of which colour set to buy is an important one – that's why we've taken an extra space on the next page to tell you all the facts about TRINITRON.

Sony Trinitron colour TV – you won't believe it until you see it

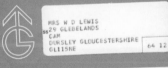

This TV for Hire/Purchase

With the World Cup no more than four years away, now is the perfect time to upgrade your rental TV set to a new colour model. You might even consider waving goodbye to your coin-slot set along with Radio Rentals, and welcoming home a sleek teak 13-inch beauty of your very own.

You'll be thrilled to discover you're getting a real bargain, too. In the unimaginably distant future year of 2019, you'll be able to look up 1972 prices on your home computer and discover that £192.30 has the equivalent purchasing power to £2,516.33 in 21st-century money.

In other words, buy now instead of waiting 47 years and you'll make a saving of over £2,300!

Let's take a look at more of the features and benefits of becoming a modern TV family:

1 – One new bar scarf courtesy of the lady in your life.

2 – A year's subscription to *Shoot!* mag. Or was it a comic?

3 – One junior Arsenal kit.

4 – Matching rosette and bobble hat (other teams are available).

5 – One secondhand 'caser' football. Mum's plantpot and table lamp, beware!

6 – One pint of fizzy bottled keg Double Diamond to help get over the impact on your wage packet.

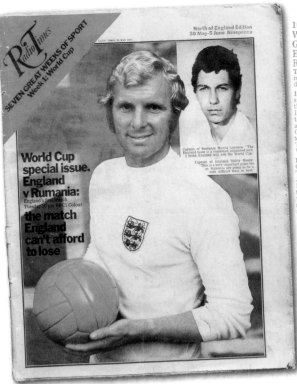

North of England Edition
30 May–5 June Ninepence

World Cup special issue. England v Rumania:
England's first match Tuesday 10 pm BBC1 Colour
the match England can't afford to lose

10.40 *Colour*
World Cup Grandstand England v Rumania
The whole of England's opening match in the 1970 World Cup, direct by satellite from Mexico.

10.40 David Coleman sets the scene for tonight's big match in the Jalisco stadium in Guadalajara. Interviews from the England team's HQ in Guadalajara, plus analysis and comment from the *Grandstand* experts, including JOE MERCER and DON REVIE.
The latest news on tonight's other World Cup matches in Mexico.

16.50 England v Rumania
Commentator DAVID COLEMAN
The whole match live from the Jalisco stadium, Guadalajara. England begin their defence of the World Cup against the country regarded by many as the outsiders in Group 3. Yet Rumania are still rated among Europe's strongest footballing nations.

12.45 Highlights of tonight's two other World Cup matches.
Peru v Bulgaria (Group 4)
Commentator
KENNETH WOLSTENHOLME
Uruguay v Israel (Group 2)
Commentator HARRY DAVIES
With comment and analysis from Mexico, and from the *Grandstand* team of experts with FRANK BOUGH in London, BRIAN CLOUGH, NOEL CANTWELL, IAN ST JOHN, RAY WILSON, BOB WILSON, JOHNNY HAYNES, WALLEY BARNES and JIM FINNEY.

Production team:
In Mexico: SAM LEITCH, JACK OATEN, ALEC WEEKS, JOHN MCGONAGLE, JIM BUMPHREY, RICHARD TILLING, JONATHAN MARTIN, ROY SHREWSBURY, JOHN MCNICHOLAS.
In London: ALAN HART, BRIAN VENN, FRED VINER, BILL TAYLOR, DAVID KENNING.
Presented in co-operation with Telesistema Mexicana and the European Broadcasting Union.
Executive producers
BRYAN COWGILL and ALAN CHIVERS

3.0 Closedown

Skipper and cover star: Mircea Lucescu knew how to make the most of his big moment.

£1.50

EVERTON VERSUS NOTTINGHAM FOREST
19th January 1992

LEAGUE DIVISION ONE

THE LIVE MATCH OFFICIAL MAGAZINE · NUMBER 8

IAN ST JOHN PREVIEWS 'THE MATCH'

GEORGE GRAHAM MANAGER'S VIEWPOINT

BRIAN MOORE TV'S TOP COMMENTATOR

WIN A TRIP TO THE MATCH OF YOUR DREAMS

WIN England v France tickets with TENNENT'S PILSNER

ISSN 0960-8206

World Cup Special

INSIDE: Your pull-out passport to Argentina

MAY 27–JUNE 2

LONDON July 9–July 15

TV TIMES/6d

WORLD CHAMPIONSHIP · JULES RIMET CUP · ENGLAND · 1966

SEE THE WORLD CUP ON ITV

sign of the times

NORTH 21–27 May 1977 Price 12p
BBC Radio Sheffield: page 64

Up for the Cups!
It's the climax of the football season on BBCtv and Radio, with the FA Cup Final at Wembley on Saturday and the European Cup Final in Rome on Wednesday. Inside: young fans talk about the magic of the game.

The Live Match Mag

ITV Sport's short-lived *The Match* magazine might take a bit of explaining to younger readers. It's one of those football curiosities that seems counterintuitive – like when your mate tells you he's got the FA Cup final programme from when your team got beaten by Liverpool in the '80s, and you have to break the news that it's not a rarity. It's barely worth a quid in back-pocket condition, 'cos every newsagent in the country was selling them. Yes, the same ones that were on sale at Wembley.

Before *The Match*, the only mags mining the exciting live football/TV coalface were big-match editions of the *TV Times* and *Radio Times*. They did Cup finals and World Cup finals – that's it.

But then in 1983 ITV secured the rights to screen live League matches. There was no need to go to Goodison Park. You could eat pie and drink beer and moan with your mates on the sofa.

The only thing missing on the retail front was the chance to get a programme. So stay-at-home punters snapped up *The Match*.

Imagine if they produced a glossy mag for every televised match today. You'd probably need a new bamboo magazine rack.

the men on the telly

Saint & Greavsie

Funny Old Game

TV football's celebrity Dark Ages didn't last long. Even before the end of the '60s the commentators, anchormen and pundits associated with the game began to assume a status seemingly at odds with the simple job of saying who was playing, who had scored and who had just been nutted on the thigh by Billy Bremner.

It wasn't enough just to watch the game on telly. We had to be led behind the scenes and taught the finer points. By experts.

The football annuals came first, and any hoarder of a certain age will have relatively inaccessible bookshelves packed with titles such as *David Coleman's World of Football*, *Kenneth Wolstenholme's Book of World Soccer* and Jimmy

Hill's *Great Soccer Stars*. We'll have to give this dark, scary underworld its own section next time.

There were pundit-centric LPs and commentator casualwear, too, because the birth of TV soccer celebrity didn't stop at books about Tony Gubba balancing on the gantry at St Andrews.

Did you know ITV anchorman Dickie Davies launched his own range of smart-but-casual slacks and jackets? What price now an original 'DD' logo sports shirt on the booming mod revival revival market? We're also hoping

our Merit World of Sport game (audaciously based on Magic Robot) might be worth a few bob, for purely selfish reasons.

Aside from Brian Moore's readable *The Final Score* autobiog, the cream of the telly merch has to be Saint & Greavsie's *Funny Old Game, Football* LP. Let's not forget, their TV clips 'n' chat show was a groundbreaking, killer format. And there's no surer way back to 1987 than via banter, football singalongs and (gulp) dance remixes with sampled anecdotes.

A WHOLE NEW BALL GAME!

FA Premier League Football
LIVE only on SKY Sports

First 15 customers to buy a system will receive a mystery Premier League gift.

UPFIELDS SATELLITE CREDIT DEAL

Philips 256 Satellite only £329.99
including installation worth £79.99 and redundancy and accident cover.

NO DEPOSIT and nothing to pay until January 1993.
36 monthly payments of £14.72 **OR** 24 monthly payments of £19.38
(Total Credit Price £529.92) (Total Credit Price of £465.12)

A.P.R. 34.4% Monthly Rate 2.5%

These offers are open to customers who subscribe to both Movie Channel & Sky Sports

14 High Street
Botley
Tel: 0489 785004

6 The Locks Heath Centre
Locks Heath
Tel: 0489 885122

Service Centre, Unit 3
28 Butley Road, Hedge End
Tel: 0489 784027

SKY SPORTS

UPFIELDS ARE A LICENSED CREDIT BROKER

ANDY GRAY

Andy Gray took tactical analysis to a new level in Sky's 'Boot Room'.

A Clean Break with the Past

"Two years ago, the face of English football was changed forever by the creation of the FA Premier League..." This is Andy Gray talking, in his introduction to the first ever Merlin Premier League sticker album, in 1994.

"A clean break with the past, a new competition, has proved the catalyst for further innovations in the English game. Today we can enjoy a new form of live TV coverage in the shape of Sky's fresh approach, in which yours truly is proud to play a part. Now, here in your hands you have the very latest product of this new football world. This wonderful collection does for football collectables what the Premier League itself did for football as a whole."

No, not that.

"It, too, breaks with tired, old conventions – the very first of a new tradition, which will be looked upon in years to come as truly a landmark in football collections. As the saying goes, it's a whole new ball game!"

Well, it was certainly the first time we'd seen stickers featuring a 'stedi-cam', TV commentators or a Sky Sports Zeppelin.

There were Sky facts, too: 'Ian Darke and Martin Tyler each commentated on more than 40 matches. That's the same as talking non-stop for three whole days!'

In fact, it isn't quite the same. But no quibbles with this next gem: 'Richard Keys is known as "Rainbow" by the rest of the Sky Sports team because he wears a different trendy brightly coloured jacket at every game.'

Now we want to sign up for Sky Sports to see more of what fans are calling 'a whole new ball game'. We hope we get one of the 15 mystery Premier League gifts.

Fever Pitch came with two alternate covers, in a love v football battle.

Fever Pitch (1997)

Nick Hornby's autobiographical novel was enormous in the '90s. It deftly encapsulated the humour and frustration of obsessive football fandom within the Trojan horse of an equally perceptive romantic comedy. Or maybe vice-versa. Either way, it was perfectly timed to capitalise on football's new-found acceptability.

It took five years for the film to emerge, with Hornby himself projecting his own quirks and one-liners on to the big screen, via affable Colin Firth. Debutant director David Evans did a TV-ish

job, guiding the ball safely down the middle to ensure a tap-in finish against a defenceless public.

But does it stand up today?

"Arsenal were fucking rubbish last year. They'll be rubbish this year, too. And next year. And the year after that. I'm not joking."

"I don't know why you come, Frank. Honest I don't."

"Well, you live in hope, don't you?"

When Saturday Comes (1996)

An enjoyable kitchen-sinkish trawl deep into the parks-league mentality of Sean Bean, washed-up goalbanger who coulda been a

contender. There's beer, curry and Sheffield angst aplenty, plus Emily Lloyd and Pete Postlethwaite to keep the spirits up.

Any football fan will struggle to watch this underdog tale without a secret empathy. Putting yourself in Jimmy's boots. Looking back on that old school-team promise... the modern-day beergut, and wondering... *what if?*

Bend It Like Beckham (2002)

This gently subversive film by Gurinder Chadha was way ahead of the curve. Casually hijacking the brand name of England's sexiest superstar, it shocked many

Gone South: Derek's long wait to catch Robert Duvall at Palmerston Park.

goals on film

blokes with the curious idea that women could play football. Cleverly, it also allowed everyone to pretend they knew all along.

Well, you wouldn't want to end up on the side of the well-meaning but culturally outdated characters who try to prevent Parminder Nagra (or Keira Knightley) fulfilling her footy destiny, would you?

The Miracle of Bern (2003)
This one sticks in the memory as one of the great football films, not just because of director Sönke Wortmann's knack of shooting live action and making it look real,

but also for its ambitious reach. The personal. The social. The big match. Sacha Göpel plays a German star on a collision course with the Hungarian champs in the 1954 World Cup final; meanwhile, young Louis Kamroth is his mascot, struggling with his dad's return from a Russian POW camp.

A Shot at Glory (2000)
It seemed like a football film with all the perfect ingredients. A proper actor: Robert Duvall out of *Apocalypse Now*. An irresistible setting in the Scottish Second Division. Locations reported

online to include Palmerston Park, home of our beloved Scots minnows, Queen of the South. A cameo from Ally McCoist to lend it the pro-celeb vibe of *Escape to Victory*. And Michael Keaton who used to be Batman. What could possibly go wrong?

To get some idea of the possibilities, watch the cinematic trailer that's still up on YouTube. Those accents. That cliché. And that one, too. And Ally's acting. And most of the footy being shot at bloody Boghead Park, Dumbarton. And that final, ominous trailer credit: Music by Mark Knopfler...

Quality Treats

It's often said that new advances in technology are driven by the demand for ever more realistic pornography. We're talking photography, home movies, cable television, video, the internet, social media, virtual reality...

However, as we're a family catalogue, we'd like to put forward an alternative suggestion, that tech has always seemingly been devoted to letting us watch the best bits of our favourite football matches whenever we please.

In the smartphone age, there's a feeling that something hasn't really happened unless it's captured on a selfie/Facebook post/YouTube video/the 10 O'clock News.

Tracing this phenomenon back via reverse technological leaps we land in 1966, when every football magazine produced in the wake of England's World Cup win offered

Super-8 footage of the final along with the plummy-voiced *Goal!* documentary on reel-to-reel tape.

Why? So that we could check it had really happened.

The same phenomenon began to occur with FA Cup finals and even subsequent World Cups where the winning teams didn't even feature any well-known English players.

Super-8 tapes were selected from mag adverts placed by 'Quality Products'. Delivered under plain wrapper. Enjoyed in darkened, smoky rooms. By men lucky enough to know someone with a projector. Come on, England!

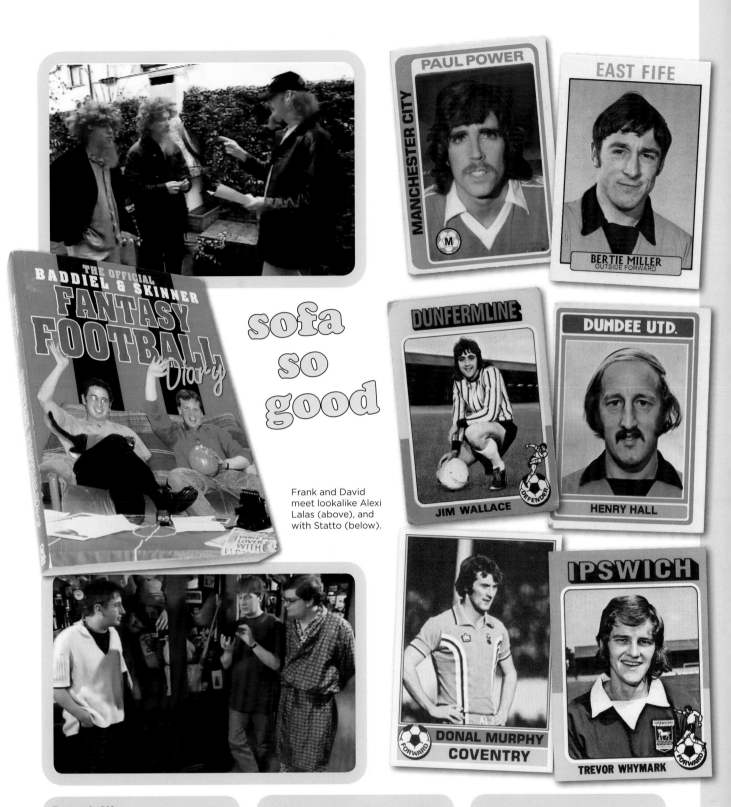

sofa so good

Frank and David meet lookalike Alexi Lalas (above), and with Statto (below).

PAUL POWER — MANCHESTER CITY

EAST FIFE — BERTIE MILLER — OUTSIDE FORWARD

DUNFERMLINE — JIM WALLACE — DEFENDER

DUNDEE UTD. — HENRY HALL

DONAL MURPHY — COVENTRY — FORWARD

IPSWICH — TREVOR WHYMARK — FORWARD

Fantastic Life

Fresh from their respective stand-up triumphs – Frank's Perrier Award, Newman & Baddiel's 'new rock 'n' roll' comedy tours – Fantasy Football was Baddiel & Skinner's TV pay-off. Absolved from the high anxiety of endless rehearsal required to hone a stage act, the show was '90s lad-era heaven for the stars. But it took sharp scripts, great research and a wealth of live experience to pull off a show this apparently easy-going. It was best early on when fantasy football was still more important than the sketches, teaching fans a new appreciation of the game once we acknowledged other teams.

Stars of Stage & Screen

If anybody out there remembers The Onion Bag from the '90s, we'd like to apologise for the infantile, offensive rubbish we used to put out on the mag's 'Say Cheesy' pages of supposedly amusing football card and stickers.

From back in the day, here's Robert de Niro of Cov, Quentin Tarantino in his Ipswich days and René out of 'Allo 'Allo! when he played for Dundee United.

Andy @ScotsFootyCards still keeps up the sick tradition on Twitter. Richard Beckinsale, Ben Stiller and Robert de Niro, this time of East Fife, are up among his recent personal best.

Swansea City

From Town to City

In July 1969, Prince Charles, the brand-new Prince of Wales, stood outside the Guildhall in Swansea and announced that the town was, at long last, to become a city. However, the Queen didn't provide the official documents until 15 December, causing havoc for the club in the midst of the 1969/70 season. Pity the poor old programme editor who was forced to ditch one cover design, then phase in the change to City – via a touchingly modest neutral period.

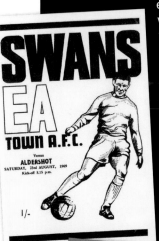

Tottenham Hotspur

Lapel Époque

In contrast to the classy, timeless message of a vintage enamel badge, the tin pin variety has a definite low-rent feel. However, there's still a ready market for the transient puns, insults and star shout-outs that constituted the prime subject matter of the golden-era pin badge. In just the same way that comic free gifts and

BAB stickers can have intense personal value despite having once been thought disposable, 'Spurs Rule Olé' brings precious memories of Ossie and Ricky flooding back.

Watford

On the Buses

This splendid Budgie Models No.706 Routemaster Bus in Watford FA Cup final 1984 livery is in mint condition. Unlike the real thing. Jon Moonie recalls a trip with the Junior Hornets for a

a fraction lower than the height of our bus. There was a sound of very loud crunching and a shout of "GET DOWN!" bellowed by youth team goalkeeper David James, and we all ducked. The roof above the first three rows

tour of Highbury Stadium on From the Rookery End's History of Watford in 100 Objects. "We went under a railway bridge,

was concertina'd back." Miraculously, no one was hurt and the Junior Hornets got another tour – of a police station.

WBA

Sheer Class of '79

The Baggies' centenary year of 1979 was quite an occasion for the club. Aside from sparking the appearance of countless quality mementoes

in the Club Shop, and a cavalcade of after-dinner speeches by former players who had lit up the Hawthorns over the previous 100 years, the present-day side achieved West Brom's best League position since a runners-up spot in 1954.

Ron Atkinson's side's third place in the top tier hasn't since been pipped, earning the 1978/79 line-up a special place in fans' hearts. Led by long-serving skipper John Wile, it included Tony 'Bomber' Brown, who that season became the club's all-time top League goalscorer; future England captain Bryan Robson; the trailblazing trio of great black players, Cyrille Regis, Laurie Cunningham and Brendan Batson; legendary Scots winger Willie Johnson; and the season's top goalscorer Ally Brown.

It must be a pleasure to take a slice of commemorative cake and reflect on the sheer class of '79.

West Ham United

Big Chevron

What an introduction to Admiral! Having made it to the 1976 ECWC final in a traditional Bukta claret-and-blue, West Ham ran out against Anderlecht in this one-off version of the following season's new kit, which sported collar logos and a special central badge.

The chevron shirt ruled until 1980 and has remained a firm favourite ever since.

Wolves

A Giant Step

It was one of those Eureka! moments that would go down in history. When an absolute absence of creative inspiration was suddenly jolted with an idea of godlike status.

Yes! That was it! The Wolves programme editor lit a fat cigar in celebration. This season's big cover theme was sorted at last: he would present the lads of Molineux as gods...

Here's Andy Gray in divine mode, looking down in exasperation from on high as mere mortal Andy blasted an easy chance over the bar. Shame, also, that there wasn't much of a crowd in to see giant Andy leaping out of the John Ireland Stand, but at least one young fan got a chance to worship the omnipotent George Berry.

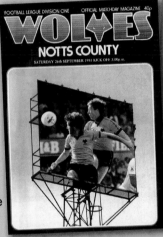

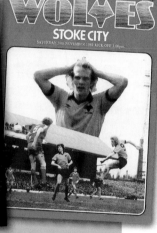

In his moment of inspiration, the prog ed even had a prophetic vision of John Richards on a futuristic Jumbotron screen. Yes, it was up a floodlight pylon; but it's still technically a miracle.

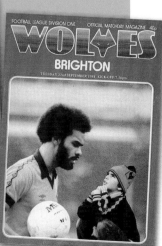

The final touch: Magnificent Leeds United tracky... with bonus stirrups!

Track Best

The tracksuit is a rare example of perfection in sporting design, a triumph at the intersection of form and function. Name another item of kit that features stylish go-faster piping in a choice of upwardly aspirational logos; a built-in temperature regulation system, and zip-up ankles. You can't, because the tracky is unique.

Dress a footballer for practice in a two-piece tracksuit and he instantly presents a positive model for club and crest. Get a tracky for Christmas and it puts out the right message about a junior wearer: a smart, dedicated athlete intent on self-betterment up the park.

So where did it all go wrong?

First came the kit v clobber divide. Replica tracksuit tops were so ineffably cool, every herbert on your street wanted to wear one all of the time. The tracky became a mere cardigan, too often deprived of its nether companion. Next, grown men took to leisurewear as an alternative to smart-but-casual.

And now the travesty at the modern Premier League training ground, where professionals are filmed going through their paces wearing not only shorts with ankle socks but also hi-vis jackets and sports bras concealing microchips.

Heavens above, what would the great tracksuit managers say about the post-tracksuit age?

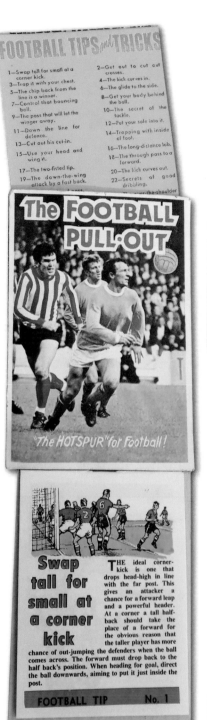

tip-top tips

Do As We Say...

Playing football and going to the match are the only times a proper soccer kid feels fully alive – no matter when said infancy occurred nor whether said infant has since achieved grown-up status. The problem is getting through the other 99% of our waking hours.

Games and comics, stickers and books helped to conjure an imaginary world of football before it became wall-to-wall football on the TV and internet. And they still can. Even today, there's nothing like an expert training tip or tactic to set the imagination reeling with optimistic visions of beckoning superstardom.

Learn to brace your body for a barge. Don't smoke behind the bikesheds with Bobby Moore. Pull gently, and swap tall for small at a corner kick. Go on, give it a go!

Many happy weeks of my childhood summer holidays were spent studying the arrows and diagrams in soccer annuals' instruction pages. Mimicking the barely recognisable stars on the back of Anglo 'Play the Game' football cards, I mastered the exact way Rod Marsh's hip seemed to slip out of joint mid-overhead kick. Master the half-volley. How to run without the ball.

After my Clark's Commandos anguish, I could hardly believe my luck when Mum snagged me a pair of Clark's Attackers from the Cut-Price Shoe Shop in Oadby. If anyone out there ever made sense of the punch-hole Computer Coach system, please do write in. It's never too late to learn.

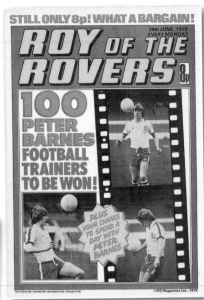

Flexi Fitness Training

Before you start training with a ball, you need to get fit with Kevin Keegan and Shredded Wheat. 'Sitting with front legs straight, other leg in hurdle position, press gently over front leg, then repeat with the other leg in front'. Got that? 'Follow a strict diet on the day of the match. No stodgy fish and chips!'

In the '70s Tizer, the luminous red fizzy pop, was sold chiefly in chippies, marketed optimistically as 'the Appetizer', though it earned its alternate soubriquet, 'the Surprizer', when Derek Dougan was signed up to help chip- and fizz-fed children become international footballers.

The flexidisc booklet is not the best-known medium for passing on soccer skills, requiring a cordless Dansette record-player to be lugged up the park. Nevertheless, that's how The Doog chose to pass on his heading tips based on the clever idea of suspending a football from the ceiling on a length of string.

The flexi flopped but the string idea proved to have legs...

Balls on String

The concept of tying a ball to your shorts with a length of string first came to real prominence in the '70s with Man City winger Peter Barnes' infamous Football Trainer.

All you had to do to learn to beat full-backs as comprehensively as Barnes himself was to practice for long hours with the lightweight ball tugging at the elastic on your shorts. If they'd only allowed this deceptively simple training aid on the field of play, the England side of the '80s might have looked very different, full of former devotees.

Into the '90s, Les Ferdinand's Kickmaster system bore close resemblance to the home-made Football Trainers many kids had previously put together using their nylon-net ball bag. It was, in many

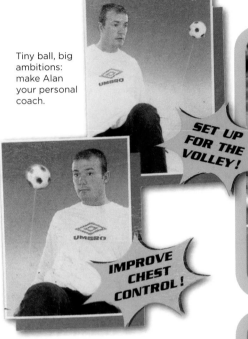

Tiny ball, big ambitions: make Alan your personal coach.

SET UP FOR THE VOLLEY!

IMPROVE CHEST CONTROL!

PRACTISE HEADERS!

ways, the 'ultimate practice partner' for soccer kids with a secret urge for solo self-betterment – but only up until the arrival of Alan Shearer's game- (and life-) changing Volley Blaster.

One of football's great lost inventions, Alan's ball on a string was only available via the side of the box containing the Shearer Shoot-Out! game. The sensational new pocket soccer trainer didn't

just help you practice headers and maintain ball control, but also to improve chest control and set up for the volley. And that was just for starters.

Alan Shearer's Magic Motion

If you've ever fancied making a weaving run through a helpless Brazilian defence, just like Alan Shearer, there's only one game that can teach you how.

Shoot-Out! commands premium prices on the rare occasion one comes up for sale. Even then, you're bidding against the financial power of Britain's top clubs, eager to turn the handle and learn the secret of Alan Shearer's magical skills. In next to no time, they too will be able to literally weave their way around the oppo.

Priceless hint: it's all down to the big magnets in little Alan's boots.

The Object of the Game

It might be stating the obvious, but football wouldn't be much of a game without the, ah, football. Given its centrality to proceedings, it's surprising that relatively few collectors attempt to overcome the sheer impracticality of a roomful of balls, each one stubbornly confirming the storage inefficiency of the dusty, part-deflated sphere.

Luckily for us, Rob Filby has got loads of famous match balls – so let's allow him to talk us through a selection of favourites from his collection.

1 – "Adidas Tricolore. The 1998 World Cup ball was the tournament's first to feature more than two colours. Intriguingly, it was also the first Adidas ball used at a World Cup – a run which began in 1970 – *not* to have been made in France. The Tricolore was made in Morocco. Bizarre, given that France was the host nation."

2 – "Adidas Telstar. Despite what it says on the ball, this is in fact the model used for the 1976 European Championships. The tell-tale clue lies in the 'Made in France' lettering, which appears on the right-hand side of the brand name, 'adidas'. The 1974 World Cup balls had the same place of manufacture located centrally under the 'das'. Lazy day at the Adidas design department, I reckon...

"'We need to design a ball for the '76 European Championships.'

'Meh, let's just use the same one as in 1974!'"

3 – "Slazenger Challenge. The ball made famous for its use during the 1966 World Cup (although this particular one was the star of Bristol Rovers v Arsenal in January 1967). Most of the Slazenger Challenge balls you see feature the name, which branding in fact marks them out as retail balls. Up until 1974, branding

wasn't allowed on balls used in World Cups so they were like this one, free of any distinguishing name or logo."

4 – "Adidas Tango. Had to include this one, because everyone loves a Tango! First introduced in the '78 World Cup, with the Tango Durlast, this is the last Tango to be used in a major tournament. The Tango Europa featured in the 1988 European Championships in Germany."

Plastic Passion: the greatest non-leather ball in the history of childhood.

a load of balls

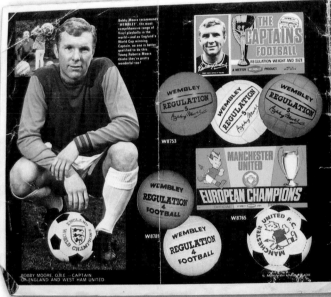

Playing Ball

In contrast to the thrill of playing with a ball once kicked by past greats – whether a specific match-played ball or merely the exact model – there's a different range of discreet nostalgic pleasures to be derived from the good old plaggy playtime special.

Has there ever been an image loaded with more latent potential, bittersweet yearning and sense memories than a load of old balls?

Feast your eyes over any range of footballs in an old catalogue or brochure and you're instantly ten again, automatically evaluating which would be the best ball,

the most expensive versus the cheapest, the best value for your mum's money, and the ones you'll do well to dodge (our apologies for those foolish, misshapen eggs).

What was the football of your youthful dreams? Was it an archaic triple-panelled bladder ball, shiny brown or white for about five minutes before the wear and tear began? Was it a more modern leather inspired by futuristic satellite design? Or one of the plastic playground staples of the '60s, '70s and '80s?

Do you remember the infinite promise of a brand-new Wembley Trophy, freshly unpacked from

its box? Pump it up with the adaptor tucked away in a small brown envelope, and you were up and running. Do you remember the sandpaper texture; the fresh plastic smell; the authentic feel of the prince of plastic balls, heavy enough to withstand puncture repair with a red-hot knife?

Or did you spend your break-times, evenings and weekends in pursuit of a lighter globe, each pentagonal panel printed with the name of a First Division club?

And so to the cheap, coloured float-away balls with stippled markings. Thanks, Jimmy, but no thanks to the 'Official' version...

"The doctor gave me some strength pills to build up my muscles, but I couldn't get the flipping lid off."

Get Fit for Footy – Easy

If you're interested in wearing a
cool headband like Steve Foster
and Rambo, follow the keep-fit
demos performed by George Best
(and close acquaintance Marie
Helvin) on the 1984 LP chart
smash, *Shut Up & Dance*. Who
better than Bestie to help you hit
your goals? Look good! Have fun!
Hang out with your mates!

Just place vinyl on turntable and
bop along strategically to second-
division disco hits, pausing only to
generously assist co-exercisers.

Note: chubbier readers may need
to step back to avoid stylus jump.

Bully Beef – Intermediate

For professional football you've
got to be all-round fighting fit.

Pull on a Bullworker like
dynamic England goalie Peter
Shilton and you'll build steel-hard
muscles in every part of your
body. Your husky good looks
will be the stepping stone to an
exciting new life.

But hold on, weren't 'isotonics'
something to do with John Barnes
and his old Lucozade advert?

Pump It Up – Dead Hard

Liverpool skipper Emlyn Hughes
gives it 100% on his chest expan-
ders. Em rows his rowing machine
to France and back every morning.
He shows his handgrips no mercy,
and thrashes his musculator to
within an inch of its life.

There's no half measures in effort
or desire when you're preparing to
lead out the Reds at Anfield – or
to take on Billy Beaumont on *A
Question of Sport*.

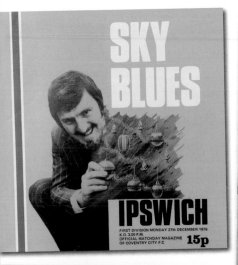

SKY BLUES

IPSWICH

FIRST DIVISION MONDAY 27th DECEMBER 1976
K.O. 3.00 P.M.
OFFICIAL MATCHDAY MAGAZINE
OF COVENTRY CITY F.C.   **15p**

IPSWICH Town

Football League
Division One
Friday December 26th 1980
Kick-off 3.00 p.m.

Norwich City

SUNDERLAND AFC
v LEICESTER CITY

40p

Canon
LEAGUE
DIVISION ONE

A Happy Christmas
to all
Sunderland Supporters

VOLUME 12   No. 12
SUN. 18th DEC. 1983
KICK-OFF 3.00 p.m.

Inside:
ROKER FOCUS ON
MARK
PROCTOR

SEASONS GREETINGS

SKY BLUE THE OFFICIAL MAGAZINE OF THE COVENTRY CITY FOOTBALL CLUB LIMITED / VOLUME ONE · NUMBER SIXTEEN

COVENTRY CITY v ALBION / 26th DECEMBER 1970 / SKY BLUE OFFICIAL MATCHDAY MAGAZINE   2

crackers!

Lane Line Up Competition

Prize Winner: Stephanie Grayson
19 Creswick Lane
Grenoside
Sheffield, S303NL

ON BOXING DAY 1972 1st DIVISION FOOTBALL AT BRAMALL LANE

UNITED

K.O. 3pm

V.

LIVERPOOL

GREETINGS

Sheffield United F.C. Lane Line Up Vol.3 No. 17 6p.
including "League Football"

EVERTON

Tuesday 26 December 1978   Kick-off 3 p.m.
Official Match Day Magazine   Price 20p   MAN CITY   Football League Division One

MUSIC CENTRES TVS
RADIOS CALCULATORS
EVERYTHING'S SHARP

Albion News

30p   Volume 72   Programme Number 18   FOOTBALL LEAGUE DIVISION ONE · SEASON 1980-1981

ALBION
v
MANCHESTER UNITED

INSIDE TODAY
GARY OWEN
COLOUR POSTER
BETWEEN THE
POSTS

Season's Greetings...

The Festive Programme

At Christmas time, many of the regular rules of football have traditionally disappeared straight out of the frost-rimmed window. And what's good enough for the fixture calendar, for playing conditions and unofficial World War I ceasefires must surely also provide an excuse for the Yuletide football programme.

Did you know that from League football's Victorian beginnings right through to the late 1950s, English clubs used to play a fixture on Christmas morning – swiftly followed up by another on Boxing Day, most often a 'return' game against the same opponents?

If the old Christmas fixture system upset countless family dinnertimes, the time-honoured tradition of players partaking of a rare festive tipple must also have been tough for the pros to take.

Not to mention the fans who were expected to travel to a game on consecutive mornings after.

In Scotland, Christmas Day games were traditionally only played when they fell on a Saturday. A full programme of fixtures last appeared on the calendar for 1976 before icy weather and hangovers saw the game count reduced to just two!

It was just such festive frolics that saw Coventry City's 1970 Christmas programme controversially coloured Santa red, a one-off hiccup in the Sky Blue tradition covering literally every

other issue these past 57 years.

The regular programme cover's usual action shots and star portraits are routinely deemed nowhere near special enough for the Christmas issue. Instead, you

get the chairman creepily peeping out from behind the club tree, a random celebrity off the telly or a hastily inked cartoon of the boss as Santa, looking suspiciously mince pie-eyed.

Favourite of all is the old trick of getting players to dress up as Saint Nick. That's Forest's Stuart Pearce

giving us a helpful clue as to his assumed identity; but pity poor old Ricky Hill and Brian Stein of Luton, gamely playing along with a 'creative' photographer's idea for an extra touch of festive fun.

As for Brighton's 1983 Santa effort, it's nearly as sinister as Watford's MkI Harry the Hornet.

Couldn't someone have told Steve Foster and the lads that clowns (especially the scary killer variety) are nothing to do with Christmas!

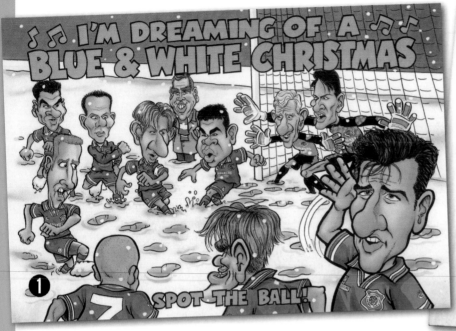

Club Class

It's easy for us to sit on the sidelines as fans and collectors, gently taking the Michael. But we must begin our festive trawl through a historical selection of genuine football club Christmas cards by admitting that we're hugely jealous of all the recipients whose names appear in the cards.

Coh, what we wouldn't give to be officially greeted by the chairman (or his secretary) and the players at any club (via photocopied scrawls) – even if most of the cards are badly misjudged, quietly controversial or just a bit crap.

Having spent hours forensically tracking down clues to seasons, characters and events, we can only conclude that you shouldn't read too much into club Christmas cards. Nevertheless:

1 – Here's Leicester's last-minute cover-up to disguise the shameful 1995 exit of boss Mark McGhee to Wolves. Steve Walsh was shifted to the front, with a random hand gesture to hide McGhee's massive nose. Incredibly, on the previous year's card, Brian Little had been supplanted by Filbert Fox, having also exited under a cloud, to Villa.

2 – In 1987, Derby County's card casually reminded fans about the Ramtique club shop – and the inevitable bumper January sale.

3 – This 1978 greeting was sent by West Ham to the other Football League clubs. But why choose this grim Dickensian vision of fans being forced to sing? Maybe in the hope of gaining favour and a few more goals at Upton Park in '79?

4 – And why was Paul Parker depicted here as a child sitting at Fergie's side – on a pudding? Top marks if it takes you less than 15 minutes to identify everyone here, from Roy Keane and Dennis Irwin to David May and him on the left.

We wish you a jolly good Xmas: Happy players, no injuries and bigger gates.

have a cool yule

5 – More Dickensian squalor, this time courtesy of Bolton Wanderers, whose naughty '90s card was later used as evidence of cruelty to this frozen street urchin.

6 – It's Rotherham, Division Four champions, 1988/89! Put the bloody elves and reindeers on hold. If you've got it, flaunt it.

7 – Southampton FC selflessly asked Santa for happy players, bigger gates and success on the field in 1962. Their results can only suggest a slight hiccup on the old fella's 'naughty or nice' test.

8 – This prized item of historic ephemera only cost £1.00 off eBay, but it could be worth 20 times that amount to any Millwall fan with a finely tuned sense of humour. Lions snowmen Theo Paphitis (off *Dragon's Den*), horrible boss Dennis Wise and assistant Ray Wilkins are in good cheer after their FA Cup final year of 2004. But Ray quit as soon as Harry Bassett came in as coach in 2005. Theo said, "I'm out." And the lone Wise man was soon to follow.

Sickness, insults, cheap props and costumes, dodgy choirmasters and a double helping of Man U. Happy Xmas, everybody.

Relatively Merry Xmas

Hats off to *Goal* mag for keeping it real and reminding us all of those less fortunate at Chrimbo time. But, bloody hell, this has to be one of the most harrowing football mag covers ever produced?

Nope. In fact, there's a long history of cover images seemingly designed to prevent Christmas mags flying off the shelves.

1 – First, that Dickensian cover shot of the less fortunate kids at Great Ormond Street Hospital. Taken not with a flashcube but with a broken 20-Watt lightbulb,

all the colour is drained out of the photo along with any sense of hope. Arsenal skipper Terry Neill tempts a sickly girl with tragically modest gifts. A teddy with a poorly head. A highwayman en route to the gallows. And beneath the gloom, a cheery strapline: a Munich Air Disaster survivor gives his Verdict on Violence.

2 – Sadly, *ROTR*'s dwindling end-of-year budget didn't stretch to a Santa hat or more than four baubles for The Doc's cheap tree.

3 – Gary Lineker learns that the greatest goalscorer of the '50s

doesn't much rate his own efforts. Happy Christmas to you, too, sir!

4 – A terrifying image of evil choirmasters Rush and Hateley with schoolboy Mo Johnston in their charge. Plus David Speedie's private fantasies about dwarves.

5 – The *Shoot!* editor's seasonal lesson in equality and goodwill: Man U get two covers stars, and to Hell with the rest.

6 – The Hockey family crouches together in the one decorated corner of their lounge, pretending it's Christmas in August. Okay, Trevor, whatever you say.

The Unboxing Feature

It was my favourite ever Christmas present, the first luxury addition to a Subbuteo stadium made mostly out of layers of cardboard glued together to form terrace steps, plus one grandstand set. In time it would be joined by St John's Ambulancemen with a stretcher, spiky fences, riot cops on horseback and the Queen.

But the TV Tower set C110 always remained special as the first touch of realism, the first sense of the outside world encroaching on my imaginary, carpet-level world.

Maybe it is a tiny bit obsessional to recreate my Christmas morning of 1975. But it rates as one of my experiences of both centuries, so I hope the innocent pleasure is contagious to fellow Tower kids.

After unwrapping the gift that I prepared for myself months ago, using genuine vintage Chrimbo paper, I start by emptying the set's familiar building blocks and ready-painted characters out of their thin plastic bag.

The tower uprights locate with a pleasing click in the base, and the twin platforms – ooh, the realistic

grainy detail on those planks! – slide smoothly into place.

Up the sturdy ladder climbs the cameraman in his regulation blue duffle coat, in plenty of time to catch the kickaround before the big kick-off. And then he's joined on the tower's sheltered first floor by the commentator himself. Barry has got three knobs to twiddle and two screens to watch, just as soon as he's donned his cans and tested his whisper mic.

Out in the OB van, the producer slips the Perspex teamsheet into view. We are ready for action.

has HE been?

Christmas Box:
Here's hoping Auntie Olive
has got the right club.

On Christmas Morning

Over the years, we've amassed a bit of a track record of appearing under the tree on Christmas morning – and here's hoping this year will keep up the Got, Not Got tradition. It isn't just prezzie recipients who let us know that Santa has been kind to them, by the way. It tends to be more their wives and girlfriends, complaining how we've helped ruin Christmas morning due to Bob/Colin/Jason

being stuck in the corner with his nose in a book, repeatedly telling his baby daughter, "I had one of them but Mum threw it out."

This is the sort of scene we love:

1 – It's Rich Smith modelling his first ever Newcastle shirt on Christmas morning, 1996/97. It's a smashah! But nevertheless upstaged by Mum's Xmas jumpah.

2 – Wee Iain Clark makes his long-awaited debut in the orange and black of Dundee United. Don't

worry, Clark Minor, your time shall surely come.

3 – Half Man Half Football Manager, @HMHBFM, looking quietly deadly in Liverpool Hitachi. "The Brucie Bonus is my brother in his Spurs shirt," he comments with barely concealed sibling rivalry.

4 – And it's the same story at Steven and Gary Chapple's house, proudly showing off their Bristol City and Man City kits, and the

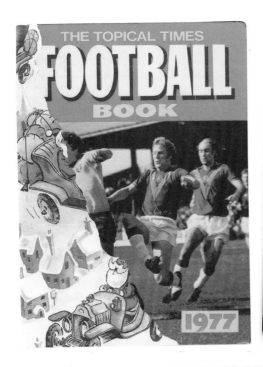

Alex parks the bus, while Bob elbows the floodlight pylon aside.

Scalextric with the Minis. Did no one's parents bring up two kids to support the same side in the '70s?

5 – It's Scott and Stewart Campbell in their respective brand-new Ipswich and Forest shirts. Hats off to dad, who must be hiding a 50 per cent secret sense of indoctrination failure!

6 – A brilliantly evocative photo capturing the thrill of a new Subbuteo set. It comes courtesy of Alex, boss of the mod-friendly Art Gallery clothing empire.

"My dear old late dad was up early with us to catch the action on Christmas morning," Alex remembers. "I'm on the right in vest and sweatbands, and that's my brother Bob on the left in his astronaut pyjamas!"

7 – And finally, it's Grimsby Town fan, goalkeeping obsessive and modern-day comedian Lloyd Griffith enjoying his moment as Peter Schmeichel back in the '90s.

The Authors

Derek Hammond and Gary Silke are the authors of *Got, Not Got*, runner-up in the BSBA Football Book of the Year 2012, and the following series of books covering programmes, kit, fans' photographs taken from the terraces and the memorabilia of many individual clubs.

Derek is an editor and copywriter who has written for publications including the *NME, Time Out* and *FourFourTwo*,

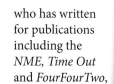

and has worked for four national publishers. Derek is the singer in unpop group Yeah Yeah Noh, John Peel's favourite new act of 1984.

Gary Silke is a journalist and designer with long editorial experience, having produced *The Fox*, one of Britain's first football fanzines, for over 30 years. He has written a weekly column for the *Leicester Mercury* since the '90s.

Gary and Derek founded Conker Editions in 2017, an imprint specialising in books on football, memories and memorabilia.

Acknowledgments

Peris Hatton, @toy_toys_shirts on Twitter – real football, real vintage football shirt collector/dealer extraordinaire. Thanks for sharing so many amazing shirts; Neville Evans and Simon 'Shakey' Shakeshaft at the National Football Collection; Karl Hanssens for access to a wonderful historic photo archive; Nigel Mercer, proprietor of Nigel's Webspace, the number 1 '60s/'70s football card resource; Andy@ScottishFootyCards; Thomas B. Ramsden & Co. Special thanks to Christine for helping to secure our permission to use the wonderful cover knitting pattern; Graham Convey – thanks for all the impossibly rare A&BC material; Barrie Farrell and the Admiral kids – Left to right: Jonathon Mullholland (Wales away), Paul Wishart, Barrie Farrell (Coventry home), Ross Farrell (baby), Mary Mullholland and Alan Mullholland (Wales home). The photo is from July 1977 and was taken in Kirkby, Merseyside; The UK Computer Museum, Cambridge.

Visit www.computinghistory.org.uk and the fantastic museum. Thanks for the console pics; Andy Ellis for the archive pics; Paul Woozley at oldfootballgames.co.uk; Miles McClagan @TheSkyStrikers; Rob Stokes, author of *Glove Story*; Paddy@90sfootball; Alex Banks at ArtGalleryClothing.co.uk, for all your modernist needs; Lee Gray, proprietor of the Kop Locker FB page; Mark Baxter, co-author with Paolo Hewitt of *The Fashion of Football* – Thanks for the catalogue trainers page; Craigleith Art and Design – check out footballmodels.moonfruit.com; Gavin Haigh; James Hills; Chris Bignall; Martin Bennett; Neil Pearce; Dean Nelson; Bill Hern; Iain McCartney of the United Review Collectors Club.

Picture Credits

Many thanks to everyone who sent images to us, Got, Not Got books are truly a huge collective effort.
Paul Woozley – Teams display 13, Big League 77; Pete Blackman – Seaman 14, Shirts 99; James Hills – 16, 17; Craigleith Art and Design – Hibs 19; Paddy @90sfootball – Blackburn 25; Clinton at Chunkywestham eBay shop – Everton 21; Neil Dunham – Watford 21, 113, 117; Graham Denton – Villa 22; Michael Kennard – 23; Ben's Bargain Barn, Fizzy_b123 eBay shop – Blues 24; Patrick Morgan – Bristol Rovers 26; Dave Price – Bristol Rovers 26, 95, 96, 110, 116; Andy Ellis – 8, 27, Shilts 29, Derby 127, 144; Sue Williamson – Lineker 29, Bobby Smith 76; Richard Mitchell – 30; Steve Mitchell – Leeds 32, Films 140; Karl Hanssens – Man U 34, 74, Car 77, 80, 81, 82, 83, Villa 85; Anthony Heywood – Man City away 34; Antony Cooke – Braces 35; Andy Starmore – Leeds 35, 38, 82; Dave at enchantedspace eBay page – Walsall 38;

Ron Crane – Burnley bus 50; Sam at futuresailor28 eBay page – Celtic 50; Ron Fraser – FKS collector 66; Steve Marsh theyflysohigh.co.uk – West Ham 76, 156; Mark Wilbraham – 79; Richard Greenfield – Wivenhoe 83; Neville Chadwick Photography – Leeds 87; Roger Pashby – Huddersfield 87; Malky @TheDonsPool – Hibs 87, Aberdeen 90, Scotland 93; Chris Simm – Hearts shirt 87; Barrie Farrell – 88; Matthew Lumb

eBay page – QPR 114; Stephen Millar, The Rangers Archive @oldrangersvideo on Twitter – Rangers 114; Offside Sports Photography, welloffside.com – 117, 118; Paul Billson, billsygreenfox on eBay – Villa 117; Keith Murphy – Ipswich 119; Paul Owens – 121; James at spacecity80s eBay page – Clock 121; Mike Gurr – Leicester 123; Howard Tomlinson – 123; LawnLegends.co.uk – Billy McNeill 123; Andy McConachie – Derby 124; Chris Hinsley – Leicester 124; Neil McNair – West Ham 124; Pete Hurn – Films 140; Andy @ScotsFootyCards on Twitter – 141; Nicholas Martin Diecast – Watford 142; Rodney George – West Ham 142; Rob @bobso1902 on Twitter – Balls 150; Simon Kimber – Background 153; Rich Smith – 160; Iain Clark – 160; Half Man Half Football Manager, @HMHBFM – Liverpool 160; Steven and Gary Chapple – Man City v Bristol City 160; Scott and Stewart Campbell – Ipswich v Forest 161; Alex Banks – Subbuteo 161; Lloyd Griffith – Xmas tree 161; Wayne Tomlinson – Panini letter 163.

– Barnsley 96; Hinson Chung, @thepredatorpro on Instagram – 100, 101; Rob O'Donnell – 102, 103; Eddie Sparrow, MCFC Memorial Let's Not Forget Past Blues Facebook page – 102; Jonathan Wheatley – 102; Thanks to Tosh at Heritage Unlocked, @HeritageUnlockd on Twitter – Cup 103; Stu Hancocks – Man Utd 103; Dave Morcom Photography – 105, 133, 163; Rob Stokes – Gloves 99, Shredded Wheat 108, Pompey 114; Robert, scrappy1968

Teamwork...

Robert Wheeler - Arsenal FC

Terence Ryan -
Wolverhampton Wanderers

Simon Sheldon - England 82

John Pietralski -
Bolton Wanderers

Alan Thompsett -
Arsenal FC & Crawley Town

Martin Rockley

Ishmael Lewis

Martin Knox

Michael Biskup

Wayne McNally -
Newcastle United

Roy Clark

Henryk Cynkar - Leicester City

Alan Appleby

Graham Marsden -
Leicester City

Phil Redmond - Everton FC

**Richard Johnson (The Football
Attic) -** Coventry City

Mark Beagan

Philip Kirk -
Bury Town FC (Suffolk's finest)

Mark Henshall

Michael Saville

Lucas Dance - Leeds United

Jonnie Dance - Leeds United

Wayne Bullock

Craig Matthews

Liv and Matt Hale -
Come on you Baggies!

Darren John Barnes -
CF14 BLUES

Dominik Robbins -
Newport I.O.W.

Howard Tomlinson -
Manchester United

Alasdair Ross - Ipswich Town

Emil Anderson

Diane Potts

Anthony Cox - Coventry City

Alan Whybrow - Birmingham City

Stephen Halliwell -
Wigan Athletic

John Keningale -
Tottenham Hotspur

Paul Barton - Coventry City

Andy Collier

Duncan Lewis

Ian Brown - Stoke City

Rob Stokes - Portsmouth FC

Andy Ellis - Derby County

Shroppie Mon - Shrewsbury Town
#monarmy #salopianation

Marc England

Martin Bennett -
Southampton FC

Mark Anthony

Robert Bugter - Go Ahead Eagles

Mark Wilcox

Rich Barlow - Leeds United

Martin Jones

Peter Snashall

Stuart Hargreaves

Dave Dinsmore

Ray Webb - Chester FC

Jonathan Darley

Matthew Lumb - Barnsley FC

Malcolm Stark

Cliff Wagstaff

Stuart Hancocks

John Hague

Wayne Tomlinson -

Doncaster Rovers

Neville Evans

Simon Shakeshaft

Teresa Waterman

Paul Bowser - York City

Paul Hughes - Birmingham City

Brook Miller - Columbus Crew SC

Stephen Varley

Roy Cunningham

Lynne Harrison

Peter McNally - Manchester City

James Hills

Dave Clayton -

Queens Park Rangers

Steve Lawrence

Luke Earnshaw

Andy Judd - Ipswich Town

Jason Chapman

Susan Davis

Colin Perry - Manchester United

Graeme Waite

Paul Leeson - Leicester City

Philip Darwin - Swindon Town

Neil Emslie -

Stirling Albion & Sunderland

Andy Collon - Luton Town

Billy Pointer - Norwich City

Gary Stinson

Ken Herts - Leicester City

North Stand Critic -

Portsmouth FC

Karl Hanssens -

Manchester United

Andy Lowe

Dave Phillips - Leamington FC

Derek Bell - Berwick Rangers

Matt Braddock

Mike Albiston - Crystal Palace

Paul Steele - Fulham FC

John Morley

Neil MacLeod - West Ham United

Stewart Henry - Leicester City

Max Henry - Leicester City

Noah Henry - Leicester City

Peris Hatton

Max Gassner - FC Nürnberg

Bill Hern - Sunderland AFC

David Warren - Fisher FC

Dean Wade - York City

Gavin - Liverpool FC

Bent-Roar Hansen

Neil Prentice

Kevin Rinchey - Aberdeen FC

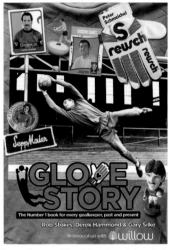